CarTech®

Grumpy's Toys

THE AUTHORIZED HISTORY OF GRUMPY JENKINS' CARS

DOUG BOYCE

CarTech®

CarTech®, Inc.
838 Lake Street South
Forest Lake, MN 55025
Phone: 651-277-1200 or 800-551-4754
Fax: 651-277-1203
www.cartechbooks.com

© 2011 by Doug Boyce

All rights reserved. No part of this publication may be reproduced or utilized in any form or by any means, electronic or mechanical, including photocopying, recording, or by any information storage and retrieval system, without prior permission from the Publisher. All text, photographs, and artwork are the property of the Author unless otherwise noted or credited.

The information in this work is true and complete to the best of our knowledge. However, all information is presented without any guarantee on the part of the Author or Publisher, who also disclaim any liability incurred in connection with the use of the information and any implied warranties of merchantability or fitness for a particular purpose. Readers are responsible for taking suitable and appropriate safety measures when performing any of the operations or activities described in this work.

All trademarks, trade names, model names and numbers, and other product designations referred to herein are the property of their respective owners and are used solely for identification purposes. This work is a publication of CarTech, Inc., and has not been licensed, approved, sponsored, or endorsed by any other person or entity. The publisher is not associated with any product, service, or vendor mentioned in this book, and does not endorse the products or services of any vendor mentioned in this book.

Edit by Scott Parkhurst
Layout by Monica Seiberlich

ISBN 978-1-61325-299-4
Item No. CT489P

Library of Congress Cataloging-in-Publication Data

Boyce, Doug.
  Grumpy's toys : the Authorized history of "Grumpy" Jenkins' cars / by Doug Boyce.
    p. cm.
  ISBN 978-1-934709-27-6
  1. Jenkins, Bill. 2. Automobile engineers—Biography. 3. Drag racers—United States—Biography. 4. Dragsters—United States—History. I. Title.

TL140.J46B69 2011
796.72092—dc22
 [B]
                                2010024392

Written, edited, and designed in the U.S.A.

Cover:
This photo was taken at the World Finals in Dallas, the final NHRA points race in 1970. Both Dave Strickler and Bill Jenkins were on hand competing with Grumpy's 1969 Camaro and this 1968 SS/RS car powered by 430 inches of aluminum Chevy. The number "101" denotes Dave Strickler as the current driver who is looking great here on his dry hop. Dave fell to eventual winner Ronnie Sox in the second round. (Photo Courtesy Ray Mann Collection www.quartermilestones.com)

Fronticepiece:
At the 1969 NHRA Winternationals, the Camaro ran SS/D and won its class, but bowed out in the first round of eliminations to Jerry Harvey's SS/I 428-powered Mustang. (Photo Courtesy Bob McClurg)

Title Page:
Jenkins catches some air coming off the line at Numidia Dragway. (Photo Courtesy Harold Hoch)

Back Cover:
Bill Jenkins forever changed the face of Pro Stock drag racing with his revolutionary 1972 Vega, captured here at New England Dragway. (Photo Courtesy Paul Wasilewski)

Foreword by Bill Jenkins..6
Preface..7
Acknowledgments..9

Chapter One: The Beginnings..10
The Making of Grumpy Jenkins..11

Chapter Two: Dave Strickler and the *Old Reliable* Cars............15
Old Reliable I, 1961..15
Old Reliable II and *Old Reliable III*, 1962....................................21
Old Reliable IV, 1963..29
A Strong *Northwind*..35

Chapter Three: The Chrysler Years: 1964–1965..........................38
The Dodge Boys, 1964...38
Bud Faubel's Honkin' Dodges..48
Black Arrow Plymouth, 1965..49
Monster Mash Chevy: The Original Grumpy's Toy?.....................55

Chapter Four: Super Stockers: 1966–1969..................................60
Grumpy's Toy I, 1966 Chevy II..60
Grumpy's Toy II, 1966 Chevy II...64
Grumpy's Toy III, 1967 Camaro..65
George Cureton's *Tokyo Rose*..71
Grumpy's Toy IV, 1968 Camaro..74
Grumpy's Toy V, 1968 Chevy II...83
Dave Strickler's *Old Reliable*, 1968 Camaro................................88
Grumpy's Toy VI, 1969 Camaro..89

Chapter Five: The Pro Stocks: 1970–1983...................................98
Grumpy's Toy VII, 1970½ Camaro...98
Grumpy's Toy VIII, 1970½ Camaro..100
Grumpy's Toy IX, 1972 Vega...109
Grumpy's Toy X, 1972 Vega..118
Grumpy's Toy XI, 1974 Vega...129
Grumpy's Toy XII, 1975 Monza...136
Grumpy's Toy XIII, 1976 Monza..141
Grumpy's Toy XIV, 1977 Monza..147
Grumpy's Toy XV, 1979 Camaro...151
Grumpy's Toy XVI, 1981 Camaro..156
Grumpy's Toy XVII, 1983 Camaro...161

Chapter Six: Beyond the Toys...163

Epilogue..170

Appendix..171
Index...174

Foreword by Bill Jenkins

I received a call from Doug early in 2009, telling me he was in the middle of writing a book based on my career in drag racing. He mentioned that the cars would be the focus, and asked if I'd mind answering some questions. Initially, I questioned the relevance of such a book, but went ahead and offered up answers to any questions he had. After countless conversations, here we are.

Reading through the completed work, I realized that from the angle in which it is written, those with an interest in the cars and my career would want to read this book. It captures the highlights in detail, and I believe it presents more to the average reader than what they've come to expect out of similar books. To a point, this book eliminates the unnecessary rhetoric and the usual "BS" that follows it.

I can say that Doug has done his homework. He's done a good job of putting into words the information that I have shared and has obviously gone to great lengths to interview countless people to ensure the story he was writing was as accurate as time, memory, and recorded history allowed. Over the years, I've lost track of a number of the people Doug spoke with, so it was good to hear from them and read their recollections of events.

When I started my career 60 years ago, there was no way I could have imagined the path it would take—from the early stock cars through Pro Stock and Competition Eliminator. The Pro Stock Truck program was another good deal but, in the end, it had too many things going against it. I guess it's obvious to say now, but the sport of drag racing has been good to me. It's allowed me to live a comfortable life doing what I enjoy doing.

It's an old cliché, but you're only as good as the people you surround yourself with and over the years, I've had the opportunity to work with some good people. Joe Tryson, who, outside of a couple years in the service, was with me for 35 years. Steve Johns, who we hired out of high school, was with me for more than 20, and current shop foreman Jake Barbato has been here for 12 years now. These are just a few names that have helped establish Jenkins Competition, making it what it is today.

I've been asked many times about when I was going to sit down and write another book. Well, this is probably as close as it's going to get. I want to thank Doug for the extensive effort he has put into the book and for taking the time to tell the story as it is.

Bill Jenkins
January 2011

Preface

I became interested in drag racing during the early days of Pro Stock and, in my world, the sun rose and set on the Chevys of Bill Jenkins. If you're a Chevy fan, you know what I mean. It was kind of like the old E. F. Hutton television commercial; when Bill Jenkins talked, everyone listened. It really didn't matter if your allegiance was with Chrysler, Ford, or AMC; *you knew* he knew what he was talking about.

Bill has been described by his peers as a genius. He takes the guesswork out, approaching each build methodically. Every move, every change was the result of forethought. He knew how to make gobs of horsepower, and could tell you how each one was gained.

His contributions to the sport have included the first Pro Stock tube chassis, the first McPherson strut in Pro Stock, the first dry-sump oiling system built specifically for drag racing, the first kick-out oil pan, the electric cooling fan, gas ported pistons, piston volume enhancing groove, carburetor vibration dampener, and the slick shift transmission. All of these innovations are used in one form or another today.

I was introduced to Bill in the spring of 1975. He made an appearance at our local airstrip-turned-drag strip to run a match race against Dick Landy. Somehow, our local hot rod association, the now-defunct C.H.R.A., had convinced them both to make the trek out to the boondocks and put on a show.

That day, Bill and his Vega defeated Dick Landy and his Dart, besting him two out of three. If it wasn't for catching a red light in the second run, I'm sure it would have been a clean sweep.

I followed Bill's career into the 1980s, until I married and started raising a family of my own. Drag racing took a back seat for a number of years but, now that the kids have grown, I'm back into it. Seeing the way in which the sport has progressed over the years makes me realize how much I miss the old days. When did the Pro cars stop looking like cars, and where did all the electronics come from?

The purpose of this book is to document the history of Grumpy's *Toys* and other cars of Jenkins Competition, and what I regard as his career highlights. I wanted to go behind the scenes and find answers to questions that most interviewers had never thought to ask or had never reported.

This book is not meant to be a technical breakdown of each component of every car. If this is what you're looking for, you may be disappointed. Over the years, enthusiast magazines have done a great job of taking a technical look at most of the *Toys* and Bill himself has released a couple very informative books that are worth searching out: namely the *Chevy Power Guide* (released in 1971) and *The Chevrolet Racing Engine* (first printed in 1976).

Here is the author at age 13 ruining an otherwise great shot of Ken Dondero, Bill, and **Grumpy's Toy X.** *(Photo Courtesy Dave Boyce)*

Preface

Sadly, not everything has been documented over time, and relying on memory alone can be challenging. The information in this book has been confirmed, usually more than once. There were a few recollections omitted because they either did not coincide with documented history or were not fit for print. Thankfully, there were few cases of either.

Attempting to trace the 60 years that Bill Jenkins has been involved in drag racing has, for the most part, been a pleasure. It was frustrating at times, but looking forward to the end product was always a great way to keep the motivation alive. Like a kid on Christmas Eve, sleep would not come in anticipation of the next day's interview or mail delivery. It was always great discovering new information and dispelling old myths about the man and the cars.

It was a pleasure talking to and interviewing the old-time and not-so-old-time racers, those who were there and involved in what I view as the golden age of drag racing. The stories they told could fill another book, and maybe someday they will. These men enjoyed reliving the glory days as much as I enjoyed hearing about them.

Almost every person I talked with stressed the importance of downplaying the "Grumpy" moniker. They say it really was nothing more than a gimmick. If Bill seemed grumpy to the average spectator, they were misinterpreting his focus on the task at hand. Through the multiple interviews with Bill, I found him to be nothing but cordial, open, and honest. While I'm sure he has been given reasons over the years, he refused to speak ill of anyone.

The frustrating part of writing this book was not being able to get through to those whom I had hoped would share a memory or two. I can only assume this was due to previous bad experiences with the less-scrupulous-journalist types in our society. Though there were very few downsides to writing this book, one of the more painful was discovering how many of our racing heroes had passed on. Sadly, their stories have not been told.

While compiling information and photos, the majority of the people I talked with were more than eager to help in any way they could. To me, this spoke volumes about the type of people involved in this sport. It also said a lot about Bill Jenkins, a man who surely has more friends and fans than he realizes.

Bill has always preferred the mechanical ingenuity it took to build a winner, as opposed to merely getting behind the wheel of a race car. He was once quoted as saying, "It [driving] was just a means to an end." And in regards to his early Pro Stockers, "Well, any monkey could drive one of these." Though he previously described himself as ego driven, today he seems a humble-enough man.

Dean Martin once said, "Sooner or later, every great man has a good book written about him." I hope that this work is accepted by everyone who picks it up as that "good book" about Bill "Grumpy" Jenkins.

Acknowledgments

Information for this book was gathered from personal accounts, interviews, enthusiast magazines, and industry newspapers. In my youth, I waited at the newsstand for delivery of the latest issues of *Hot Rod, Car Craft, Popular Hot Rodding, Super Stock & Drag Illustrated,* and more. These fine magazines were invaluable when it came time to gather and confirm information. Special thanks for the memories go out to all those photographers, writers, and editors.

Bill Jenkins, thank you for the years of entertainment. Thank you for your time, patience, and approval. Your approval of this book matters the most to me.

Without my wife, Laura, and her continuous support, patience, and belief, I would have never seen this project through. You encouraged me to carry on during the low points. Thanks for believing.

Thanks to my older sibling, David, who instilled the car bug in me all those years ago. This hobby has been a curse and a blessing to me…and it's all your fault!

Additional credit and recognition goes to the following, for, without their written words, recollections, and photos, this book would not be. To those I may have overlooked, trust that it wasn't intentional.

Herb Anastor, Sam Auxier, Jr., Jake Barbato, Derrick Von Bargen, Steve Bell, Dave Bishop, Larry Brinkley, Darren Boyce, Robert "Doc" Burgess, Francis Butler, Al Carpenter, Terry Cook, Phil Cooper, George Cureton, William Curley, Russ Dodge, Ken Dondero, Tom Doniphon, doverdragstrip.com, John Durand, John Eichinger, J. S. Elliot, Ronnie Evans, Bud Faubel, Bill Floyd, Verne Frantz, Joe Gardner, Pete Gemar, Mike Goyda, Ed Hedrick, Harold Hoch, Pete Hutchinson, Richard Hughes, John Jadauga, Steve Johns, Kevin Johnson, Tom Kasch, Roger Lamb, Joe Lepone Jr., Sam Marino, Bob McClurg, Jim McFarland, Dick McLaughlin, Doug Mentzer, Michael Mihalko, Thomas Nagy, Joel Naprstek, Mary Pizzi, Jim Pizzi, Bob Plumer, Rob Potter, Pete Preston, Hayden Proffitt, Ed Quay, Bob Rice, Clark Rovell, Carl Rubrecht, Tom Schiltz, Steve Scott, Roger Sinistri, Pat Smith, Bill "Spider" Spanakos, Geoff Stunkard, Ron Sperry, Jere Stahl, Rick Stief, Mike Strickler, Charlie Strunk, the NHRA, Jim Tice Jr., Bill Truby, Bruce Tucker, Carlo "Ollie" Volpe, Paul Wasilewski, Les Welch, Todd Wingerter, and a special thanks to the many board members of the H.A.M.B. message board (www.jalopyjournal.com).

Unless otherwise noted, sources for reference have included Argus Publications, Lopez Publications, Petersen Publications, *Drag News,* and *National Dragster.*

Finally, I give special thanks to the good Lord for giving me all that I have, and Ma, still missing you.

With its optional, lightweight, and high-revving 265-ci small-block churning out 195 hp, the 1955 Chevrolet forever changed drag racing. Bill knew a good thing when he saw it, and was in line early to get one. With 4.11:1 gearing and a three-on-the-tree manual transmission, the little Chevy would turn low-16-second quarter-mile times. (Author Collection)

Chapter One

The Beginnings

William Tyler Jenkins, "Bill" to you and me, was born of Welsh descent in Philadelphia, Pennsylvania, on December 22, 1930, and was the first of two children for Martha and Clayton Jenkins. At the tender age of 5, Bill began sharing his parent's love and affection with a baby sister. Bill's mother was a full-time homemaker, spending her days tending the home and raising the two children, while his father supported the family. He earned a living as an architect, putting his touch to such structures as the renowned Ben Franklin Bridge in Philadelphia.

When Bill was 11, the Jenkins family pulled up stakes and moved from the bustling metropolis of Philadelphia, 30 miles northwest to the sleepy mill town of Downingtown in the county of Chester. Though drag racing would afford him the ability to travel the world, Bill never moved far from Philadelphia, choosing to live his entire life within a 35-mile radius of the city.

The Beginnings

The Making of Grumpy Jenkins

Bill loved to tinker, and out of this developed an interest in all things mechanical. By his early teens he was toying with and repairing tractors and combines for local farmers in the community. By age 15, he graduated to working on the service truck of a local International Harvester dealer.

Airplanes and trains captured his imagination early in life, and his interest in the railroad stayed with him through his later years. He subscribed to rail-related magazines for a number of years and could tell you which locomotive was zipping by, just by the sound of its whistle.

Prior to earning his driver's license at age 16, Bill purchased his first car, a Model A Ford. Yes folks, the man who would forever be known for his Chevrolets started his driving life behind the wheel of a Ford. Though he only owned the car for six months or so, it was the start of his lifelong interest in the automobile.

Bill completed his schooling, graduating with honors from Downingtown Senior High in 1949. His yearbook was a forecast of things to come when it stated "Watch out for Jenkins' Chevy."

Not much of a "bat and ball" guy, Bill prefered the French Club, photography, and stage productions through his senior year. He made his one and only big-screen appearance in 1958, when members of the West Chester Modifiers car club, to which he belonged, appeared as extras in the movie *The Blob*. This classic B movie filmed in Downingtown and starred the late Steve McQueen.

By his own account, Bill wasn't much of a bookworm and, above all else, his interest in cars and the opposite sex took precedence, and not necessarily in that order. As his reputation and ego grew throughout the following decade, Bill developed a bit of a reputation as one who liked to chase the skirts.

After graduating from high school, Bill attended New York's Cornell University sporadically through the mid 1950s, studying to be a mechanical engineer. In later years, he voiced his disappointment in not having pursued this path in life. He felt that if he had, his impact in the automotive field may have been greater.

In the fall of 1955, Bill quit Cornell for good because his head was no longer in it. Sadly, his father had recently died and this, in combination with a shortage of funds and the beckoning of the booming automobile industry, helped make the decision to quit easier.

His illustrious drag racing career began in October 1953, behind the wheel of a 1951 Chevrolet that he had won in a country raffle. Dissatisfied with the lack of power produced by the stock 216-ci inline six, Bill gradually upped the power by installing the usual 1950s hop-up items to boost performance. A stock 216 bottom end only takes so much abuse before expiring, and that's just what happened. Having to replace the engine anyway, Bill took the opportunity to step things up a notch by installing a fully rebuilt, hopped-up 235-ci mill.

After impressing the local "in-crowd" with the car, Bill caved to peer pressure and traveled the 250 miles to Manassas, Virginia, to make his first trip down a drag strip. The 1/5-mile dirt track was not much of a strip, but on the East Coast, circa 1953, a person was hard-pressed to find anywhere to race legally. Pennsylvania would not have its first drag strip until the airstrips at Allentown and Lancaster were approved for use in 1954–1955. Bill was a natural at the sport, winning the equivalent of C/Gas honors his first time out. "This was too easy," he thought, and it would be another year or two before he'd go back.

Feeding the mechanical genius and car nut within him, Bill went to work for Usher Oldsmobile in Downingtown. Like a sponge, he absorbed and retained all things mechanical. The same year, Bill rented a couple garage bays in the town of Exton and opened "Jenkins Competition Tune Up Service." To pay the rent, Bill split the profits with the owner of the building.

In the fall of 1954, Chevrolet released its revolutionary 265-ci V-8 engine and the hot rodding world

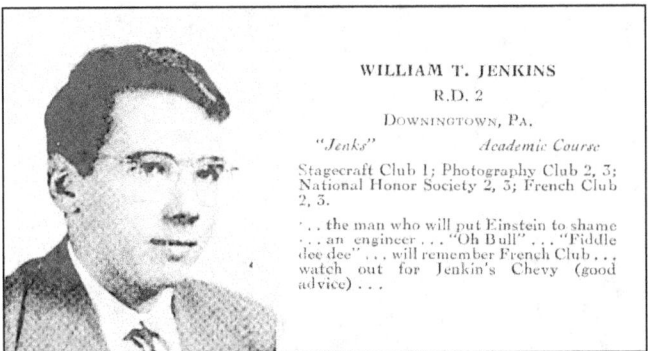

The Downingtown High School Yearbook said it all: "Watch out for Jenkins' Chevy." Bill graduated in 1949 with honors. (Bill Jenkins Collection)

Grumpy's Toys 11

Chapter One

would never be the same. The Ford flathead V-8, which had been the hot rodder's engine of choice for the past 20 years, had been falling out of favor ever since the introduction of the modern overhead-valve V-8 in the late 1940s. With the release of Chevrolet's high-revving, compact version, the final nail was driven into the flathead's proverbial coffin.

Bill cashed in his 1951 Chevy and purchased a new 1955 Chevrolet, a two-tone green ragtop powered by the 180-hp "Power Pack" 265-ci V-8, backed by a three-on-the-tree (column-shifted manual transmission) and 4.11:1 rear axle gears. Not satisfied with the factory power output of the 265, he had the optional Corvette camshaft installed, bumping the output to 195 hp. The Bel Air won many races at the recently opened local landing fields that were turned into drag strips.

By this time in his young life, the nickname "Jiggs" had taken hold. As Bill would explain, his father was known as "Jenks" and it initially carried over. "Jiggs" was somehow derived from Junior, as in "Jenks Junior."

In late 1956, after returning from the NHRA Nationals in Kansas, "Jiggs" sat down and wrote the stock category rules for the Eastern Hot Rod Association. At the time, the NHRA had some rudimentary rules for what was then termed stock racers, based on the vehicle's weight and its advertised horsepower. These rules didn't take into account the latest horsepower offerings from Detroit and, on top of that, no Stock eliminations were run. Bill wrote classifications based on the ratio of advertised horsepower to vehicle shipping weight, took into account the current crop of performance offerings, and developed elimination rounds. NHRA director Bill "Farmer" Dismuke, who originally hailed from Connecticut, saw no problem with taking the category breakdowns and factors that Bill developed to California with him in 1960. There, the rules would be adopted by the NHRA. Over the next 14 years, we saw these rules evolve from Stock to Super Stock, and finally to Pro Stock.

Throughout 1956 and 1957, Bill continued to work at Usher Oldsmobile, perform part-time Tech duties at Lancaster Dragway, and spent his spare time tuning for the likes of Clarence Evans and his 235-ci six-cylinder Chevy-powered dragster. *The Roach*, as it was appropriately named, was a stripped-down 1938 Chevy that showed some local success running B/OG, an early dragster classification.

Regarding Bill's days at Lancaster, ex-Northeast Division One director Darwin Doll stated, "When I first met Bill, I was president of the Sportsters Roadster Association out of York. We had a 1937 Ford coupe with a Chevrolet 348-ci engine. Jiggs was doing tech inspection at Lancaster and was known as 'Mr. Tough Guy.' He caught the cheaters and moved them into the modified category in a hurry. They tried it all; domed pistons, solid cams, etc., but he caught it all; they didn't get anything by him. We had Bill tune our coupe, and when it came time to pay, I had forgotten my checkbook. He kept the slicks until we paid him at Lancaster on Saturday night, which we did, and he gave us our slicks back so we could compete."

By the later 1950s, Bill partnered with John Good in running a 354-ci Hemi-powered Crosley. This car ran as an A/Altered, turning 12-second times, and would win its class during a marathon 16½-hour race day at Lancaster.

Bill's membership card to the West Chester Modifiers, a car club that is still going strong in York County, Pennsylvania. Club members appeared in the 1958 sci-fi flick *The Blob*. (Bill Jenkins Collection)

Rose Red Timing Association certificate received by Bill after setting class record with *The Roach*. (Bill Jenkins Collection)

The Beginnings

One of Pennsylvania's first drag strips, Lancaster opened in 1954. Many cars passed through these gates, and many cars were tossed by a tech inspector who knew his stuff. Jiggs Jenkins saw it all and caught it all, bumping cars from class that did not meet the rules or regulations. (Photo Courtesy Dick McLaughlin)

A new Jersey State Police car gave up its 392-ci Hemi for the Bilbo dragster, which followed the Crosley. Pulled from a Chrysler 300C, Bill had the Hemi bored to 417 ci and topped 150 mph with it. This short-wheelbase car saw some ink on a national level, being the first gas-burning dragster on the East Coast to reach these speeds. The car was described by Bill as a handful: "It was tough trying to keep it under control as it bounced around the track a lot. And stopping? With just rear drum brakes, it was hair-raising."

Bill continued to race his own 1955 Chevy into 1958 before trading it in on a rare fuel-injected 283-ci 1958 Impala. In 1959 he loaded up the car and headed to sunny southern California to take in the West Coast's booming drag racing scene. He was happy to meet the celebrities he read about in the pages of such magazines as *Hot Rod* and the *Drag News*.

More and more of Bill's spare time was being spent performing tune-ups and repairs for locals, quickly establishing a reputation as a man with a knack for wringing the most out of Detroit's finest. By the end of 1958, he said goodbye to his day job at Main Line Oldsmobile and went into business for himself full-time, renting a bay from an Amoco station in Devon. Bill recalled that there were initially some pretty lean times

John Good in the crude-looking S&G Special. Working out of his Exton Garage, Bill assembled the Hemi for this A/A Crosley. (Al Brown Photo Courtesy Tom Brown)

Chapter One

Jiggs joined the 150 mph club in 1958 while driving John Good's six-carb, gasoline-powered 417-ci dragster. (Photo Courtesy Mike Goyda)

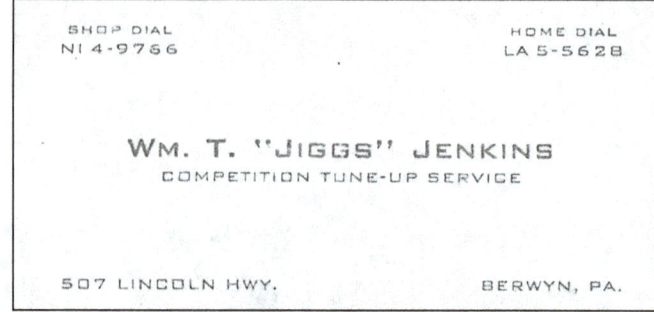

Like any new business, Jiggs' Competition Tune-Up Service had a few lean years, but his growing reputation ensured nothing but success. (Bill Jenkins Collection)

A homemade woodie followed the Crosley and ran altered with the same Jiggs-built Hemi. Drag racing was still in its infancy during the mid to late 1950s and had an almost-anything-goes mentality. (Al Brown Photo Courtesy Tom Brown)

and he took on whatever job he could just to stay in business.

During the 1957–1960 time frame, he dabbled with customer Lonnie Lowry's 283-ci, 283-hp fuel-injected 1957 Chevy. The car eventually held the record at York US-30 Dragway, with a 13.90-second run at 105 mph.

York Dragway opened in the fall of 1958. Bill occasionally worked the pits, just as he had at Lancaster prior to it being shut down in 1957 (due to complaints from the local chinchilla farmer).

York US-30 (or just plain "York," as it would come to be known) was a unique track originally operated by Bill Holtz. It was unique because it was wide enough so that four cars could run simultaneously. Occasional flagman Dick McLaughlin recalls one such evening when four stock class cars were run side by side: "Early in 1960, local 'hot shoe' Dave Strickler, in a 1959 Chevy, would go off against Bill in Lonnie Lowry's 1957 Chevy. Joining them in the two other lanes would be Bud Faubel in his Dodge and Dick Collins in his 370-ci Corvette. On this night, like many before and after, Dave Strickler got the jump on the three others and walked away with the win."

A number of years later, Dick McLaughlin asked Dave how he always seemed to get the jump on his opponent, and with a grain of salt Dave stated, "By watching the twitch in your arm, I knew when you were about to raise the flag."

The Old Reliable, lettered and ready to go. Note the stock exhaust system and the big whitewalls. Initially, the car used snow tires to get traction on the drag strip! (Photo Courtesy Mike Strickler)

Chapter Two

Dave Strickler and the *Old Reliable* Cars

How could a book on the exploits of Bill Jenkins be written without a word on Dave Strickler? The two names were synonymous throughout the 1960s. It was through Bill's early success with Dave and the *Old Reliable* Chevys that both of their names would come to national prominence. Dave Strickler's proficiency behind the wheel, his courtesy to others, and his pleasant mannerisms are legendary. Dave retired from drag racing in 1974 after campaigning a mildly successful Pro Stock Vega. He worked himself into the vice presidency of Ammon R. Smith before the doors finally closed in the early 1980s. Dave went on to work at a local dealership before succumbing to a heart attack at the age of 44.

Old Reliable I, 1961

David Ziegler Strickler was known also as "Dave," "Strick," or "Mr. 409" to some. He was born June 28,

Grumpy's Toys 15

Chapter Two

1940, in the county of York, Pennsylvania, where he would complete his schooling and live out his life. One of Dave's activities outside of drag racing was his involvement in the Boy Scouts of America. At one time, he was the youngest Eagle Scout in America, collecting more than 80 merit badges. After his retirement from drag racing, he awarded many of the trophies he had earned to Boy Scouts of America.

Like many postwar teens, hot rodding and drag racing seemed to run through his veins. In his early teens, Dave enjoyed toying with cars and taking them apart. By his admission, though, at this age he wasn't the greatest at putting them back together. By the time he was 15, Dave was racing the back roads of York in his father's workhorse Chevy truck, taking his part-time work earnings and modifying the truck by installing twin carbs and a split manifold. He eventually graduated to racing the local drag strips, honing the skills that would one day lead to 16 NHRA class Championships, 41 National Records, and a World Champion title in 1968.

Dave first met Bill Jenkins in the lean year of 1959. Dave, 9 years younger than Bill, brought his poorly running 1959 Chevy around to Bill's shop for tuning. The following day, Dave won his first trophy at York Dragway. Though Dave was no slouch with the wrenches, he continued to bring his Chevys to Bill for major tuning and tips over the next couple of years.

Dave took his first serious stab at drag racing in 1959, partnering with a friend to campaign a 348-ci-powered 1958 Chevrolet. Dave provided the 348 out of his own Chevy and *The Untouchable*, as it was dubbed, enjoyed local success.

As a new decade dawned and the Detroit performance wars continued to escalate, it became a matter of one-upmanship. By 1960, Chevrolet's Super Turbo Thrust 348 (with its 350 hp) no longer cut the muster. Chevrolet, ruling the roost since the introduction of the 265-ci small-block V-8 five years before, was suddenly left behind by the latest performance offerings from Chrysler, Pontiac, and especially Ford. Dearborn's 352-ci FE V-8 was now producing 360 hp and considered by many as the engine to beat.

Often maligned as a "truck motor," the Chevy 348-ci was designed as a big brother to the 283, a new-design V-8 engine built to power much-larger future passenger cars. In designing the 348, Chevrolet had purposely created an engine that would be suitable for both passenger car and light-duty truck use, thus the dismissive reputation. The inherited design of the 348 gave it gobs of torque, more than enough to move a large family sedan, small truck, or possibly a single-family dwelling.

In December 1960, Chevrolet responded to the competition barking at the door with the introduction of the 409. The "W motor," as the Chevrolet design team had designated the engine back in the mid 1950s, was the same basic design as the 348, but offered much more factory-equipped performance.

To handle an increase in bore and stroke, a new block was cast. Forged pistons, squeezing out 11.25:1 compression, filled the cylinders, topped by a pair of high-performance heads pulled from the 348 parts bin. The aluminum intake manifold and Carter 4-barrel AFB carburetor were additional items previously used

The still-fresh Old Reliable I *outside the Ammon R. Smith dealership. Note the green hood and scoop.* (Photo Courtesy Mike Strickler)

on the 350-hp 348. With its advertised 360 hp and 409 ft-lbs of torque, the 409 was an instant hit on the nation's drag strips, which is where most of them ended up. Because only 142 of these "Turbo Thrust" 409 cars were produced in 1961, the diehard Chevy fan was hard-pressed to find one and most would have to settle for the 350-hp 348.

The Ammon R. Smith Auto Company in York is where Dave went in search of a 409 and a sponsorship arrangement. It must have been quite the proposal; then-president Vernon Smith agreed to it and supplied Dave with the use of a 409-powered Biscayne, a tow vehicle, and spare parts. In return, the maroon Biscayne advertised the dealership by broadcasting its motto "The Old Reliable" on each flank.

It was during this time that Dave and Bill became bona fide partners and a firm handshake was all it took to seal the deal. Bill's role was to wrench, coach, and share in the driving chores when necessary. Jenkins stated that, at this early stage of their partnership, he still considered Dave a customer, but the racetrack winnings were shared equally.

At this point in his early career, Dave had already established himself as one of the East Coast's premier gear pullers, shifting the four Borg-Warner gears in his Chevy with lightning speed. Bill stated years later that he could tell Dave was a real race car driver who knew how to win. "When it came to driving a 4-speed car, nobody was quicker or smoother." Looking back, Bill said, "Dave was a good kid; a happy-go-lucky guy who never took things too seriously."

Dave's aggressive shifting style reportedly required the factory Inland shifter to be repaired numerous times. He was continuously breaking the welds.

Rounding out the drivetrain of *Old Reliable* was a set of 4.56:1 gears.

A pair of soft-compound, 5-inch-wide Bucron cheater slicks was of little help in getting the 409's estimated 400 hp to the ground, and they generally lasted no more than a weekend.

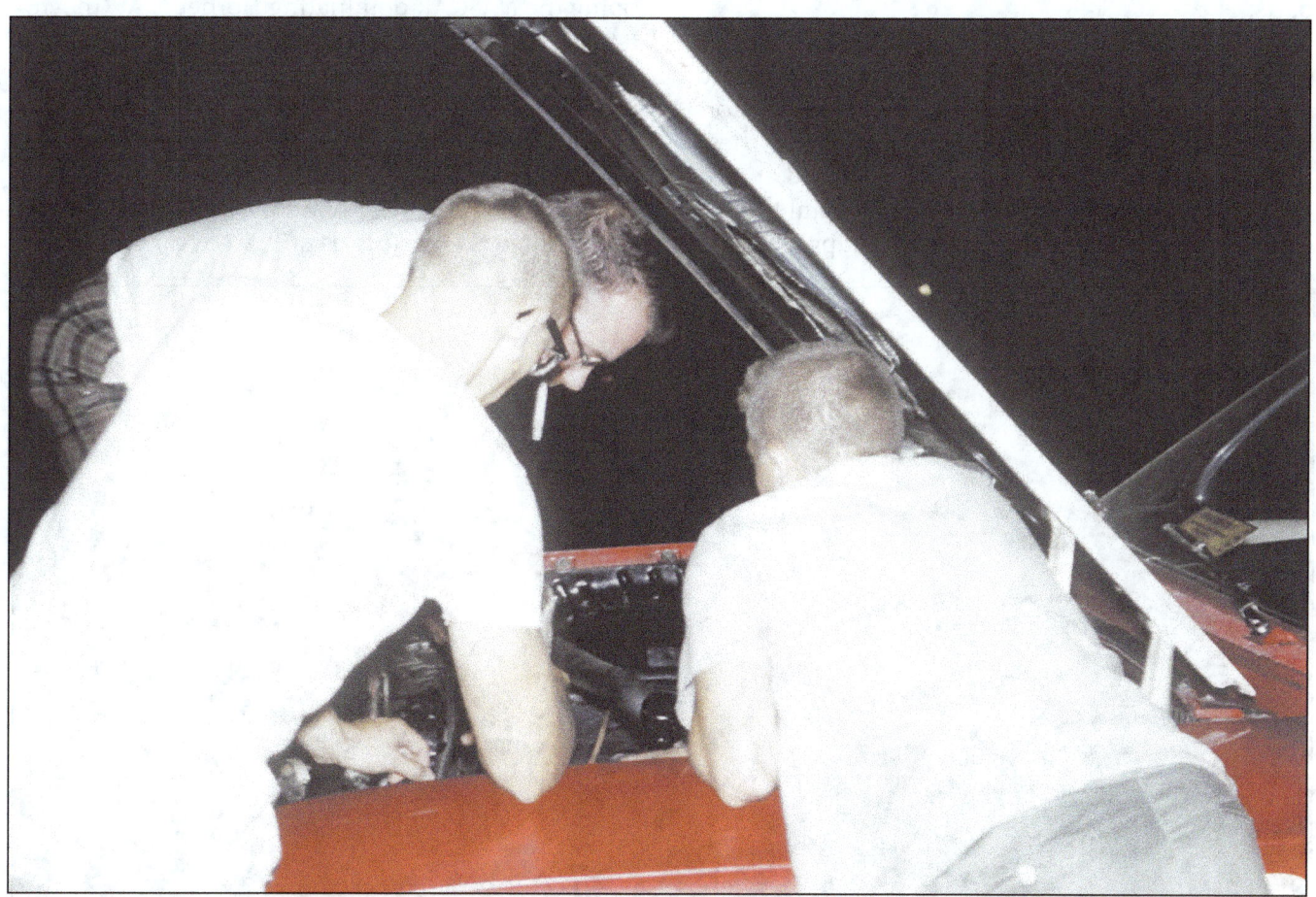

Chevrolet's 409-ci V-8 engine would all but dominate on the street as well as the Stock-class dragstrip ranks from 1961 through 1963. Bill's tuning of Old Reliable *would ensure Dave Strickler made the class finals at the NHRA Nationals.* (Photo Courtesy Mike Strickler)

Chapter Two

Jenkins did not go through the engine, as he would the later 409s, feeling that there wasn't much to be done. The carburetor and distributor were reworked, and a pair of custom Jardine headers was added.

While losing a match race to Don Nicholson down on North Carolina's Easy Street Dragstrip, the pair inquired as to who made Don's headers. It turned out his crew man, Jerry Jardine, had designed them. Strickler and Jenkins would eventually coax Jerry into making up a set for *Old Reliable*. Though noted in later photos of the car, "Sound by Miles" was nothing more than a paying advertiser, one of the few that the team could enlist in 1961. Miles Mufflers in York, Pennsylvania, is still in business to this day, operated by the original owner's son.

In June 1961, Chevrolet made upgraded performance parts available for the 409. As Bill recounted, due to a tight match race schedule, he traveled to Flint, Michigan, by himself to pick up the parts.

The over-the-counter upgrade parts included larger valve heads, a longer-duration camshaft, and a pair of deep-breathing Carter 4-barrel carburetors on an aluminum intake manifold. With these upgrades, the horsepower rating was pegged at 409.

Divisions of Chrysler, Ford, and General Motors each offered mid-year performance upgrades for their Hot Stocks. And to accommodate these cars and parts, the NHRA created the Optional Super Stock (O/SS) category. The category was designed specifically for limited production cars or high-performance parts made available by the manufacturers after June 1, 1961. The latest catch phrase, "Win on Sunday, sell on Monday" had been embraced by The Big Three and had made the voluntary AMA performance ban of 1957 nothing more than a distant memory.

Bill was introduced to Chevrolet's Vince Piggins late in 1961 by Verne Smith. As Bill described it, "Ammon Smith was a large, well-established dealership dating back to the 1920s, and Verne was well connected. He invited me along to a meeting up in Michigan with Vince."

Vince Piggins headed up Chevrolet's racing program between 1956 and 1983. Vince had joined Chevrolet after a number of years with the Hudson Motor Car Company, where he had a hand in developing the NASCAR-dominating Hornet 6. At Chevrolet, Vince Piggins and his promotions group were responsible for developing all high-performance products. Or to phrase it another way, they were responsible for the development of "heavy-duty and off-road parts." Vince Piggins practically wrote the *Chevrolet Power Guide*, which, after 30-plus years and numerous reprints, is still a relevant source of

With the service package upgrades in place, **Old Reliable** *is seen at Indy, where it ran in the Optional Super Stock class.* (Photo Courtesy Mike Strickler)

information. Through his relationship with Vince over the years, Bill had his hand in the development of many of the parts found in the guide.

In August 1961, with *Old Reliable*'s reputation well established, Strickler and Jenkins flat towed the car out to Indiana for the NHRA Nationals. Strickler defeated Arlen Vanke's 421-powered Pontiac Catalina for class honors and played runner-up to Hayden Proffitt's 12.55 at 110 mph in the Super/Stock runoff.

Hayden Proffitt described his introduction to Bill as "something else." While staging against Dave Strickler during a run up to eliminations, Hayden heard a tap on his window. Standing there was none other than Bill Jenkins. Though it would nearly cost him his hide, Bill's ploy worked and Strickler went on for the win. Hayden remarked that people like Bill and himself, guys who built their own engines and cars and could drive, were always the fiercest competitors.

In October 1961, at his home track of York US-30, Dave attended the NHRA Regional Championship drags. He drove *Old Reliable* to a 13.24-second elapsed time, setting the first-ever Stock class record. The West Coast's Hayden Proffitt, driving Mickey Thompson's 421-powered Pontiac, held the MPH mark at 109.22.

The year ended on a high note for Jenkins and Strickler; Bill moved his ever-expanding operations to Berwyn, Pennsylvania. He took over the 1,600-square-foot rear bays of Ollie Mattioli's Sonoco station out on Route 30. At the annual York US-30 awards banquet, Dave was rewarded with a certificate and a 283-ci Chevrolet engine for gaining the most individual points throughout the year. He was also awarded for having the fastest Stock car in the region.

The whereabouts (or final demise) of *Old Reliable* has never been determined, but with assistance from Bill and the Strickler family, a replica is

Photo from York. Dave waits patiently for his turn to go. (Photo Courtesy Mike Strickler)

Here's a shot from the pits of York Dragway. Note the hood scoop, an idea borrowed from the lightweight Pontiacs. Both the hood and its scoop were later painted white. (Photo Courtesy Mike Strickler)

Chapter Two

At the York Dragway NHRA regional meet in October 1961, Dave Strickler drove *Old Reliable* to the first-ever Stock Eliminator class record. (Photo Courtesy Mike Strickler)

being built. To add some authenticity to the build, they are using numerous parts that they found were removed from the original car. When completed, *Old Reliable* will be run and displayed in its former OS/S configuration.

Old Reliable II and Old Reliable III, 1962

As the new year rolled around, Bill's reputation for building winners ensured that the bays in Berwyn were always full. He hired his first employee in the summer of 1962, a young college student named Frank Hurley, to help with the everyday tuning chores. Thanks to earnings from the booming business and the racetrack winnings, Bill finally parted with his aging 1958 Impala and step up to a fuel-injected 327-powered Corvette.

A 409-powered Bel Air was special ordered from Ammon R. Smith late in 1961, to replace the *Old Reliable* Biscayne. With hopes of making the NHRA Winternationals fading fast, due to delays in delivery, a change of plans allowed the pair to pull a 409-powered car from the showroom.

Initially rated at 409 hp and developing 420 ft-lbs of torque, the engine was balanced and blueprinted. It featured the latest 1961 twin Carter 4-barrel carbs, large-port cylinder heads (modified by Bill), and power slot cast pistons squeezing out 11:1 compression. The drivetrain of *Old Reliable II* was a Hurst-shifted Borg-Warner 4-speed transmission (sporting a 2.20 first gear) and a rear end housing 4.56:1 gears. To help strengthen the notoriously weak third member, the rear center pot was drilled opposite the pinion gear, tapped, and a threaded bolt was inserted. The bolt had a brass tip built up and rode an approximate 0.005 inch off of the ring gear, eliminating excessive movement. Additional modifications included carrier cap braces and over-the-counter service-package spider gears, all of which would be used on the *Old Reliable II*, *Old Reliable III*, and *Old Reliable IV*. In examining the restored *Old Reliable II*, Bill noticed the non-original rear end, because the bolt was missing.

To get the right attitude and aid in weight transfer, a set of nine-passenger station wagon coil springs

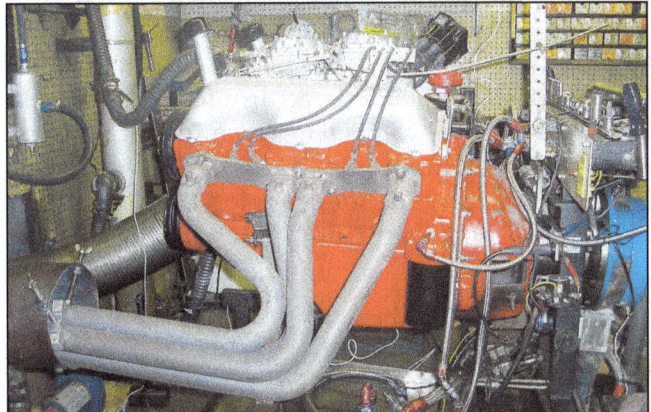

The 409 engine for the tribute Old Reliable **being checked out on Jenkins' dyno. The engine pulled over 430 horses without so much as a jet change.** (Bill Jenkins Collection)

Still without a race under its belt, Old Reliable II, **brand-new and unraced, sits prepared outside the Ammon R. Smith dealership showroom.** (Photo Courtesy Mike Strickler)

were installed up front with a set of stiffer, shorter coils in the rear. In a drastic move to improve traction, the frame mounts were relocated to almost 1 inch behind their stock location. This placed the body farther back on the frame, putting greater weight on the rear wheels, a trick for which Bill credited Ford ace Dick Brannan. To help hide the body shift from tech inspectors, the rear wheel wells were stretched an equal amount. A traction arm of Bill's own design finished out the suspension modifications.

The heart of Old Reliable II; *409 ci developing much more than the 409-rated hp. The car did leave the showroom with a heater, though it's been removed and a block-off plate is in place.* (Author Collection)

Come mid January, Strickler and Jenkins headed for sunny Southern California and the NHRA Winternationals. The first stop was a lead-up race at San Gabriel, where the Bel Air "puked the motor" on the first pass. Scrambling to scrounge up a block and pistons—2,600 miles from home—was no easy task, but eventually the pair had all they needed to build a fresh engine. Bill recalls having to belt sand the new (too large) pistons down to size, "The car ran pretty good considering the mess it was going together."

The Bel Air made it to the Winternationals, where it competed in Super Super Stock (SS/S). *Old Reliable II* set the low elapsed time of the meet with a 12.55-second pass, but lost class honors to Hayden Proffitt in his Carroll Cones–sponsored Chevy.

In the "Mr. Stock Eliminator" runoffs, Dave lost to Don Nicholson and his near-identical, Service Chevrolet–sponsored Bel Air. Ironically, some felt Dave had the title wrapped up because Don failed to make the initial call to the line. Dave came to race and Bill, who dreamed of defeating Don, made the costly decision to wait until Nicholson's car was ready. Don went on to eliminate Dave and then defeat Carol Cox for the "Mr. Stock Eliminator" title. As proof the sport of drag racing was still in its infancy, *National Dragster* reported how, in winning the battle, Don's take included a color television donated by Mr. and Mrs. Sopps of Sopps Car Wash in Los Angeles.

Heading west for the NHRA Winternationals, the pair flat towed Old Reliable *for 2,600 miles behind an Impala station wagon. The* Old Reliable *cars were all maintained at Ammon R. Smith Chevrolet in York, Pennsylvania.* (Photo Courtesy Mike Strickler)

Coming out of the chute at about 2,500 rpm, with the full weight on the rear wheels, Strickler ran Old Reliable through the gears at a reported 6,500 rpm. Dave usually relied on the seat of his pants to find the best shift point. Note Jenkins to the rear, egging him on. (Photo Courtesy Mike Strickler)

An early morning crowd gathers at the NHRA Winternationals as Strickler and Jenkins prepare Old Reliable II for competition. (Photo Courtesy Mike Strickler)

Chapter Two

Drag News reported that a few weeks later Strickler and Jenkins would be back in California for the Stock and Sports Car Drag Championship being held at Fontana Raceway (aka Drag City). *Old Reliable II* set the low elapsed time and top speed of the meet with a 12.81-second run at 113.96 mph. Unlike the Winternationals, there was no denying *Old Reliable II* this time. In an anti-climactic rematch, Dave was paired against Don Nicholson again, whose Chevy disappointed the crowd when it blew a rear axle. In the final round, Dave ran a 12.99 in defeating the Dodge of Bill Campbell.

Referring to Nicholson, Bill stated that he had a lot of respect for the man and his driving prowess. He knew, when racing "Dyno Don," there would be no starting-line antics because he was a real pro. He also said Don had a very likable personality; a man you couldn't dislike. Years later, Don briefly shared lodging with Bill and ran his 1971 Pro Stock Maverick out of Jenkins Competition. A little-known fact is that Bill prepared the Holley carburetors used by Don while winning the NHRA Summernationals the same year.

In April 1962, *Drag News* reported on one of the strangest match races of the day. The West Coast's Chris "The Greek" Karamesines, in his Hemi-powered Top Fuel dragster, took on *Old Reliable II* at York US-30. The Greek spotted *Old Reliable II* a 1/8-mile lead and still pulled him down on the top end, nipping the Chevy by inches, clocked at 9.01 seconds at 185.38 mph. The same evening, during a scheduled points meet, Dave captured top stock honors with a 12.48 at 114.41 mph.

At the NHRA Nationals in Indianapolis (traditionally held on Labor Day weekend), the Strickler and Jenkins team captured its first national event win, earning Super Stock honors by charging through six rounds of eliminations to meet and defeat their old nemesis Hayden Proffitt with a time of 12.97 to Hayden's quicker-but-lagging 12.83.

The "Mr. Stock Eliminator" runoff (which pitted the 50 fastest Super Stockers at the Nationals against one another) again found Dave and Hayden meeting up. Hayden, who had accused Dave of leaving the line too soon during the Super Stock final, exacted a measure of revenge. He eliminated Dave while on his way to the Stock Eliminator finals (Hayden later defeated Jim Thornton in the *Ramchargers* Dodge to take the "Mr. Stock Eliminator" crown).

The gang makes a pit stop in Ohio for a bite at the Beverlee Drive-In. Note the tow rigs and matching uniforms—this was the epitome of professional drag racing in the early 1960s. (Photo Courtesy Mike Strickler)

In a Petersen Publications article covering the Nationals win, Dave described how he would come off the line at the drop of the flag between 2,200 and 2,500 rpm and run the Hurst shifter through the gears between 6,500 and 6,800 rpm. Actually, Dave rarely watched the tachometer, instead choosing to drive by the seat of his pants. This frustrated the technically minded Bill; he wanted to know how the car ran, at what RPM he shifted, at what RPM he went through the traps, etc. If the car was missing a beat and Dave couldn't describe it, chances were that Bill made the next run in the car in an attempt to pinpoint the problem.

In July 1962, Chevrolet celebrated its fiftieth year in production. To help commemorate the special occasion, it produced a limited run of 20 COPO (central office production order) 409-powered, aluminum-nosed Impalas, and Ammon R. Smith was lucky enough to get two of them. Bill recalls popping the hood and how fast it sprung open. Apparently, Chevrolet had failed to replace the stiff hood springs with lighter ones to compensate for the lightweight aluminum hood

The 409 also received a late-season upgrade. Chevrolet made a dozen aluminum two-piece high-rise intake manifolds, high-lift cams with matching valvesprings, larger-port heads, and free-flowing exhaust manifolds available—over the counter. Due to the limited number produced, *Old Reliable III* raced in NHRA's new-for-1962 Factory Experimental category.

At another stop along the way. The Chevy van housed the team's spare parts, tires, etc. (Photo Courtesy Mike Strickler)

Old Reliable II *and* **Old Reliable III** *shown in the pits at Indianapolis Raceway Park.* **Old Reliable II** *was sold not long after this race, and its whereabouts today are unknown* (Photo Courtesy Mike Strickler)

Chapter Two

Some between-rounds thrashing on the Impala. It competed against perpetual competitor Dyno Don Nicholson in the Factory Experimental (F/X) class final runoff. (Photo Courtesy Mike Strickler)

Back in the day, cars were towed back to the hotel, where work usually continued into the early morning hours. This photo was probably shot the night before the finals. This photo is from Indy 1962. (Photo Courtesy Mike Strickler)

Dave Strickler and the *Old Reliable* Cars

There was little difference between the Factory Experimental (F/X) class and the previous year's Optional Super Stock (OS/S) category. It was still meant to be a place for the Detroit manufacturers to run their limited-production high-performance cars and parts. This new category consisted of classes A, B, and C, and each class was based on a weight-to-cubic-inch factor. A/FX consisted of cars weighing 8 pounds or less for every cubic inch. B/FX consisted of cars weighing between 9.00 and 12.99 pounds and C/FX was for cars that weighed 13-plus pounds per cubic inch.

Due to its heavier weight, *Old Reliable III* fell into B/FX, where it briefly held the class MPH record at 114.60. The car played runner-up to Don Nicholson's similarly equipped Impala at the Nationals, running 12.96 to Don's slightly quicker 12.93. This was the only major event that *Old Reliable III* participated in. It wasn't long after the Nationals that the decision was made to support and race only one car.

This photo was taken at York Dragway in July of 1962, and shows Dave Strickler running against John Thornton in the ex–Old Reliable 1961 Biscayne. The Biscayne disappeared from the scene after a few years and its whereabouts have never been discovered. (Photo Courtesy Mike Strickler)

Here's another shot of the "Big Go" at Indy. The legendary lightweight Impala seen with Bill and Dave. (Photo Courtesy Mike Strickler)

Chapter Two

The Impala was heavier and deemed the less competitive of the two *Old Reliable* cars. It was stripped of its performance parts and aluminum front end. Eventually the car was sold off of Ammon R. Smith's used car lot to Ralph Fischer of Pittsburgh. The car has since been rumored to be in Florida.

With NHRA's realignment of classes for the 1963 season, the *Old Reliable II* Bel Air competed in A/Stock. In January, with the newly acquired *Old Reliable* 1963 Impala still under construction, the Bel Air was towed to Pomona for the winter meet where it captured another class win with a 12.66-second pass at 114.58 mph. In July, with *Old Reliable IV* on the sidelines, *Old Reliable II* was set up to run B/FX with the aluminum front clip installed and proceeded to set both MPH and ET records at York. Later the same month, the car was match raced at Mason-Dixon and produced the first 11-second track time for a stocker. Dave and *Old Reliable II* defeated Bud Faubel's 413-powered Dodge, running times as quick as 11.86 at 120.80 mph.

At the 1963 NHRA Nationals, Dave spent most of the day bouncing back and forth between *Old*

> Ammon R. Smith
> 201 Carisle Ave.
> York, Penna.
> Presents
>
> The "OLD RELIABLE"
> 1962 N.H.R.A. CHAMPION
> Nations Quickest and Fastest
> Super Super Stock
>
> Dave Strickler   Bill Jenkins

This business card pretty much says it all! Old Reliable II *dominated its class throughout all of 1963.* (Bill Jenkins Collection)

Old Reliable II *is looking a little worse for wear in this shot, sporting a crunched fender after an accident. This was not the result of an on-track incident, but rather of falling off the trailer ramp.* (Photo Courtesy Mike Strickler)

Reliable II and *Old Reliable IV*, handling the driving chores of both. Though it had been a while since he last drove in competition, Bill was briefly called on to climb behind the wheel of *Old Reliable II* as eliminations wound down. His time away from the driver's seat had left him a little rusty, and he was eliminated in the semifinals.

In one of its final appearances, *Old Reliable II* match raced against Arlen Vanke's A/FX record-holding 421-powered Pontiac Tempest, at Cecil County, Maryland. In defeating Arlen three races straight, *Old Reliable II* turned a quick 11.73. Later in the day, Dave brought *Old Reliable II* out for an exhibition run, and banged off a crowd-pleasing 11.58 at 123.28 mph.

By the end of the 1963 season, *Old Reliable II* was transformed back to street status. Like the Impala before it, it was placed on the used car lot of Ammon R. Smith. It was quickly sold to Maryland resident John Chapel. The car passed through several owners before being purchased by current owner Larry Brinkley in 1983. Larry took on the daunting task of restoring the car back to its former A/Stock status.

During the restoration, he had to make extensive repairs to damage caused by an impetuous previous owner who had backed the car into a lamppost. During the restoration, Larry discovered the extent to which Strickler and Jenkins had gone to get the weight off the car. It was obvious that the torches had come out and anything that could be removed had been. The frame rails were drilled with lightening holes, the springs were removed from the rear seat, and, though invisible with the fenders installed, the firewall and lower cowl had sections of metal removed.

Old Reliable IV, 1963

Between December 1962 and January 1963, Chevrolet produced about 55 lightweight Z-11 Impalas, and it's believed Dave was lucky enough to get the first one. The car arrived at Ammon R. Smith's on Bill's birthday, a stormy December 22 evening. It was the only car loaded in Flint that day for delivery by Anchor Motor Freight.

Built specifically for drag racing, the heart of the $1,240 Z-11 package was the 409-derived 427-ci engine. Following the lead of NASCAR, the NHRA imposed a maximum cubic-inch rule of 427 cubes. Excluding Pontiac, which would be content to do battle with their 421, the main combatants in the factory wars either bored or stroked their performance offerings to take advantage of the new rule.

Conservatively rated at 430 hp, Chevy's 427 was a stroked 409 fitted with large-port heads, 13:5.1 compression, a camshaft featuring .556-inch lift, an aluminum two-piece intake manifold with two 4-barrel Carter carburetors, and an air cleaner housing that drew fresh air from the cowl. The Strickler/Jenkins car was one of the few cars to retain and successfully run with the cowl induction set up in place. It seemed most Z-11 owners either converted to a hood scoop or removed the inner headlights and ran cold-air ducting from the openings directly to the carburetors.

To save weight, the cars were produced with aluminum front ends and front and rear bumpers, and were delivered minus the front sway bar, heater, radio, and sound deadener. All Z-11 cars were non-SS-model Impalas equipped with the Borg-Warner 4-speed transmissions and 4.11:1 rear gears. Though

Bill makes an easy pass at the Beaver Springs dragstrip in 2002. The race was held in conjunction with Darwin Doll's Annual York Reunion show. (Photo Courtesy Larry Brinkley)

Chapter Two

Dave Strickler and Old Reliable II *at Vineland Raceway in New Jersey, in early 1963. Does anyone want to buy a quality low-mileage Chevy?* (Russ Dodge Collection, courtesy of Herb Anastor)

factory equipped with larger finned brakes, Bill replaced these with the standard Impala items which were lighter and just as efficient for quarter-mile jaunts. With final prep work, the 427 was producing in the neighborhood of 540 hp, by Bill's own estimations.

Always thinking, Bill had the underside of the car painted white; it not only reflected heat from the track surface, but it also made it easier to see when working underneath. From 1963 onward, the engine blocks were painted black to improve thermal efficiency.

The new-for-1963 alternator was replaced by a generator and, with the use of a quick disconnect running from the battery, it was used as a motor to circulate the coolant when the engine wasn't running—something that couldn't be done with an

"Aluminum, Please Touch," the fenders noted. The aluminum inner fenders were hand-fabricated, after the 1962 units that were installed disappeared prior to the current owner taking possession of the car. Note the quick disconnect on the generator. (Author Collection)

A good look at Old Reliable *at York. Note the nose-in-the-air stance. This was popular back in the day; it was felt this stance would help with weight transfer on the starting line. Limited to 10-inch-wide rear slicks, these 500-plus-hp Factory Experimental class cars needed all the help they could get.* (Photo Courtesy Mike Strickler)

With the York lights out of commission, Dave leaves hard with just a wisp of tire smoke as the starter brings up the flag. The latest Old Reliable *turned 12.0-second passes at 120 mph during the early outings at York, setting the East Coast Factory Experimental class ET record.* (Photo Courtesy Mike Strickler)

Chapter Two

alternator. The car could be shut off and pushed down the return road and cooled by allowing the water to continue to circulate. A short fan belt was used, running from the generator to the water pump only. In principle, this allowed Strickler to return to the staging lane immediately without having to go to the pits and wait for the car to cool.

Jenkins made use of the carburetors from the first *Old Reliable* because they allowed for greater fine tuning. Though the twin-carbureted 409s all carried the same part number, the front carb on the 1961 dual-quad engine differed—it came equipped with a curb idle screw.

An ignition retard system of Bill's own design was incorporated to help with the top end charge. "I had been fiddling with ways of doing that for quite some time, first making use of it on *Old Reliable II*. It utilized a vacuum tank and a vacuum advance. Drawing vacuum from the intake manifold through a check valve to the tank, you would drop it off in high gear and it would retard the timing 3 or 4 degrees."

The NHRA received its first national coverage at the 1963 Nationals when ABC's *Wide World of Sports* was on hand to record the event. The Chrondek start system (or "Christmas Tree," as it has since been known) also was introduced. Having previously installed a light system at their home track in York, experience told Strickler that you didn't have to wait for a solid green light before leaving the line. Dave was considered one of the best at reading the tree and getting the jump off the line, where so many races are won and lost.

With Dave doing what he does best, *Old Reliable IV* won its class over Ronnie Sox, barely nipping the North Carolina native with a 12.11 at 118 mph. Dave went on to take the Little Eliminator crown by defeating Jim Wangers' B/FX Pontiac with a 12.10 at 126 mph to a losing 12.61 at 108.25. Dave's big prize for his win was a high-performance 427 Ford engine, of course.

By the end of January 1963, Chevrolet had produced the required number of Z-11 Impalas, thus allowing the car to run NHRA Super Stock, with few changes.

Late in the spring, Aquasco Speedway in Maryland booked *Old Reliable* for a "bounty race." Anyone who could beat Dave that day could collect the $100 bounty placed on his head. There were approximately 20 Max Wedge–equipped Mopars on hand, along with a few lightweight Fords looking to collect. But Dave proved to be unbeatable this day, knocking off 11.90-second elapsed times while downing all comers. However, during a runoff Dave missed a shift and blew the transmission. Within a half hour a new one was in place and the car was ready to go. Bill stated that this kind of match racing was taking place all across the country. It had been building since 1958, but really took off in 1963.

At Vineland Speedway in New Jersey, *Old Reliable IV* faced off against Jim Thornton in the Ramchargers 426-powered Dodge *Candymatic*. Dave beat Thornton

The team of Strickler and Jenkins went on a rampage in 1963, making more than 200 runs on tracks across the nation and compiling a winning record of greater than 90 percent. (Photo Courtesy Mike Strickler)

Dave Strickler and the *Old Reliable* Cars

Here's a look at the top-end timing retard fashioned by Bill. It drove the competition batty. Note the black-painted surface of the distributor body. Obviously, Bill didn't stop at the engine blocks in a quest to improve thermal efficiency. (Photo Courtesy Mike Strickler)

in three straight races, a reported first for *Ramchargers*. In all three runs, Dave had to come from behind to defeat *Candymatic*. "I just couldn't hold him off," Jim Thornton said. "He [Dave] slipped by me in the last 50 feet. That car has the wildest fourth gear I've ever seen." The same evening, Dave set the track record with an 11.91-second pass at 121.62 mph.

Header man Jere Stahl rolled into Berwyn in the fall of 1963 and spent the next year working out of Jenkins' shop. Jere had built his first set of headers for *Old Reliable* the previous winter while still living in Detroit. Though crude in appearance, the headers were credited with helping the car produce its first 11-second quarter-mile time and hitting 120 mph at a Super Stock meet in York that April. Bill, who was not yet a big fan of Stahl's headers, had a change of mind after taking the car for its initial test run down a back road near Wayne County Airport. Running the car through the gears and feeling the top end pull, Bill was surprised to see a car pull out in front of him. Having nowhere else to go, he ended up on the lawn of a local resident, where he turned the yard into a mud pit while trying to get out of there. Back at Stahl's, it took a good half hour with a pressure hose to clean the mud and grass off the underside of the car. Bill was sold on the headers and, yes, it would be a number of years before he lived down the ribbing.

Once Jenkins Competition was no longer flat towing their racing cars, the 1963 car and its descendants traveled lots of miles on the back of this truck. The car is seen here prior to the NHRA Nationals in 1963. Wouldn't you love to have this setup today? (Photo Courtesy Mike Strickler)

Grumpy's Toys 33

Chapter Two

The best view from the pits of Indy proved to be from the top of a tow rig. Bill seems distracted at the moment. Maybe he's realized that he can count the total number of losses by Old Reliable IV to date on just one hand. (Photo Courtesy Mike Strickler)

MAY 25th
BIG DOUBLE SHOW
KING OF THE GASSERS — K. S. PITTMANS
PITTMAN-EDWARDS A GAS SUPERCHARGED
GOING FOR 140 mph
Will run Dragsters, Altereds
and
A Handicap match with a Super Stocker

Plus

IS IT UNBEATABLE? THE "OLD RELIABLE"

$100 Cash on the line to Any
Super Stocker or F/X that
can beat the "Old Reliable"
1 time

Want an Instant Reputation? Fame? Glory? Prestiege?
Don't hide from this one . . . Come out
* * * If you dare * * *

Vineland Speedway Drag-Strip
Route 47 Vineland N.J.

Racing track advertisements, like the car ads of the day, were always an enjoyable read. "Come out if you dare" was not an unusual challenge! It drew the drivers, who in turn drew the crowds. Though not noted here, Old Reliable II was called on to get the job done. (Russ Dodge Collection, Courtesy of Herb Anastor)

Dave Strickler and his future brother-in-law pose proudly with the winning trophy earned at the NHRA Nationals in 1963. The Hayes aluminum rims came off Bill's 1963 Corvette. (Photo Courtesy Mike Strickler)

After seeing the car's performance with the new pipes, it wasn't long before racers everywhere were clamoring for a set of Jere's totally tuned headers. As the saying goes, the rest is history.

At season's end, Dave was in search of a new sponsor. The accountants of Ammon R. Smith could no longer justify throwing its financial support behind the drag race endeavor.

Old Reliable IV was sold at the end of 1963 and the following year, the new owner, Leon Czerw, campaigned the car in the NHRA's newly formed Modified Production category.

In 1979, Bill purchased the Impala from Leon, who had parked the car 12 years before. Excluding minor wear and changes, the car was in the same condition as the day it was sold back in 1963. Bill had the paint freshened and made some exhibition runs with the car over the next few years. He sold the car in the mid 1980s, before the demand for ex-race cars inflated the prices.

Old Reliable IV has since been fully restored and is currently owned by Don and Mary Ann Fezell.

A Strong *Northwind*

Another car of prominence to come out of Jenkins' shop during this period is Joe "Tex" Gardner's 409-powered 1962 Bel Air. Joe hailed from Texas (hence the nickname) and served time in the Navy. He named the Bel Air *Northwind* after an Alaskan ice breaker that he'd served on. Joe bought the new Bel Air and delivered it to Jenkins with 23 miles on the odometer. Bill suggested the first thing to do was pull the heads and remove the extra set of gaskets that had been factory installed on all high-performance 409s. Removing the extra gasket (installed to make the engine pump-gas friendly) brought the compression up from 10:4.1 to 11:25.1. He eliminated discrepancies in compression by surfacing the heads and modifying the cylinders.

Throughout 1963–1964, Joe campaigned *Northwind* in the NHRA A/Stock category, turning times as low as 12.20 at 116 mph. The candy-apple red and gold Chevy was powered by a 0.060 overbored 409, backed by a Borg-Warner 4-speed and 4.56:1 rear

A rare shot of Vineland Speedway in New Jersey. The track closed after the 1964 season but, until that time, it drew some of the biggest names in drag racing. Here it appears Jim Thorton (in the Ramchargers *Dodge) got the jump on Dave Strickler.* (Russ Dodge Collection, Courtesy of Herb Anastor)

Chapter Two

gears. Tuning chores were handled by Jenkins' protégés Joe Tryson and Arnie Waldman, who would also spend some time behind the wheel.

Though the car failed to win on a national level, it won numerous Division One meets and consistently ran under the class record, which it held briefly with a 12.39. Joe ran the car out to Indianapolis for the Nationals in 1963 and played runner-up in class to 16-year-old Don Gay. Upon inspection, Don and his Pontiac were disqualified—the mufflers were too short! Joe's *Northwind* was also protested and disqualified because it was missing a couple of bumper brackets, which had been replaced by tow bar brackets. Such were the good old days of Stock eliminator.

Joe drove *Northwind* to Indianapolis in 1964. After realizing he couldn't compete, he made the trip worthwhile by street racing the car around Indianapolis. He quipped that he made more money than most of the guys at the nationals. He recounts that he and Joe Tryson lived in the same West Philadelphia neighborhood, where they

Dave and Bill pose proudly after their NHRA Nationals victory. Absent from the photo are the Hayes aluminum rims that were run on the front of the car. Bill has no explanation and wonders when and/or why they were switched. (Photo Courtesy Mike Strickler)

Here's Old Reliable IV *as Bill found it in 1979, complete with the Jenkins Competition logo, which was applied in 1965.* (Author Collection)

engaged in street racing on the West Chester Pike. "I guess that's where I gained my [racing] experience," he recalled.

In late 1965, with *Northwind* no longer competitive, Joe sold the car to a man in Connecticut. The 409 was quickly blown and the new owner blamed Joe for the failure. Joe bought the car back, repaired it, and raced it for a short time before selling it again, this time to a gentleman in Maryland. Joe said he was offered more money for the car than anyone in their right mind could turn down. He didn't know that the new owner would strip the car in preparation for a life in the circle-track stock car arena. In hindsight, Joe wishes he had kept the car because he really didn't need the money. "I didn't know the guy was going to make a stock car out of it."

Northwind, or what remained of it, eventually ended up in a scrap heap. Joe never owned another drag race car, instead turning his attention to the circle tracks. He owned and operated a track in Florida for a couple years before retiring from the racing world in the early 1980s.

Bill makes an easy high-11-second exhibition run in *Old Reliable IV*. *It was always one of his favorites.* (Photo Courtesy Bill Truby)

Joe Gardner's *Northwind*, *looking sharp in its red and gold paint. The undercarriage was painted white, mimicking* Old Reliable IV. (Photo Courtesy Gold Dust Classic/Bob Plumer)

The replacement for Old Reliable, The Old Goat, *seen here at Cecil County in May 1964. The lightweight Super Stock Dodge was gone by mid-summer, replaced by the new Factory Experimental car.* (Photo Courtesy Joel Naprstek)

Chapter Three

The Chrysler Years: 1964–1965

In January 1963, General Motors upper management pulled the plug on all racing activity. It was complying with the AMA ban on factory-sponsored auto racing that had been endorsed by all six American auto manufacturers in 1957. Effective immediately, factory support and products that would have allowed the team of Strickler and Jenkins to stay competitive were withdrawn. After more than two seasons of terrorizing SS/S, S/S, A/FX, B/FX, and A/S with the *Old Reliable* Chevys, Strickler made a big decision after the NHRA Nationals in September. He decided to pursue a chrysler factory deal for the coming season.

The Dodge Boys, 1964

Bud Faubel, who operated a Chrysler dealership in Chambersburg, Pennsylvania, and campaigned a

The Chrysler Years: 1964–1965

factory-backed, Jenkins-tuned Dodge of his own, played a key role in Dave receiving a factory deal. As Bud recalled, "Dave approached me late in 1963 and asked if I would talk to Chrysler's Frank Wylie on his behalf." Frank initially balked at the idea because there was a factory-supported racer (Bud) in the region already. Bud persisted on Dave's behalf and eventually convinced Frank that signing Dave would be beneficial to Chrysler; Dave campaigned his cars nationally, thus maximizing exposure. Bill had his own take on the deal, stating he caught on later that the purpose of the whole deal was to keep him from running another Chevrolet. It was a way of eliminating the competition.

Chrysler had hoped to get Jenkins' signature on a release ("We only signed drivers to contracts back then," Bob Cahill told me), but when it came time to sign, Bill was uncomfortable with the wording and refused to put his signature to it. The advertising team (who handled the budget at the time and wrote the contracts with the racers) was reportedly upset over the fact they could not use the Jenkins' name. His refusal to sign the release didn't seem like an issue to Bill; the monies paid would be going through Dave Strickler.

Apparently it wasn't too much of an issue. That December, Dave headed for Detroit to pick up his first Dodge and announced to the drag racing world that he would be switching affiliations for the forthcoming season. *Drag News* reported on the Chrysler deal, stating the initial investment was $40,000. This supplied The Dodge Boys with a shop full of spare parts, a new Super Stock Dodge, and a fully loaded, 426-powered, four-door extended-cab tow rig.

Though Dave campaigned a total of four different factory-backed Dodges between 1964 and 1965, in five different configurations, only three were in collaboration with Bill.

The first *Dodge Boys* car was a 425-hp, 426-ci, Stage III Max Wedge Polara. The car was one of 50 factory-built lightweights, and featured thin-gauge fenders, hood, doors, deck lid, bumpers, and brackets. This was a 4-speed-equipped car (would you expect anything else for Dave?), which ran Super Stock and initially produced times in the high-11-second range.

In January, Bill prepared *The Dodge Boys* car (along with Bud Faubel's *Honker* Dodge) for a trip to the West Coast to attend the AHRA and NHRA winter meets. Jere Stahl, who continued to occupy a corner of Jenkins' shop, helped to prepare the cars and build headers for each. Stahl later stated, "We were typically a day late and a dollar short, so the last few days were spent working around the clock to get the

For Strickler and Jenkins, seen here with their truck full of goodies, Christmas returned on a cold February day. Dave's crew cab was powered by a 426-ci Wedge, and came with every creature comfort available at the time. (Photo Courtesy Mike Strickler)

Grumpy's Toys 39

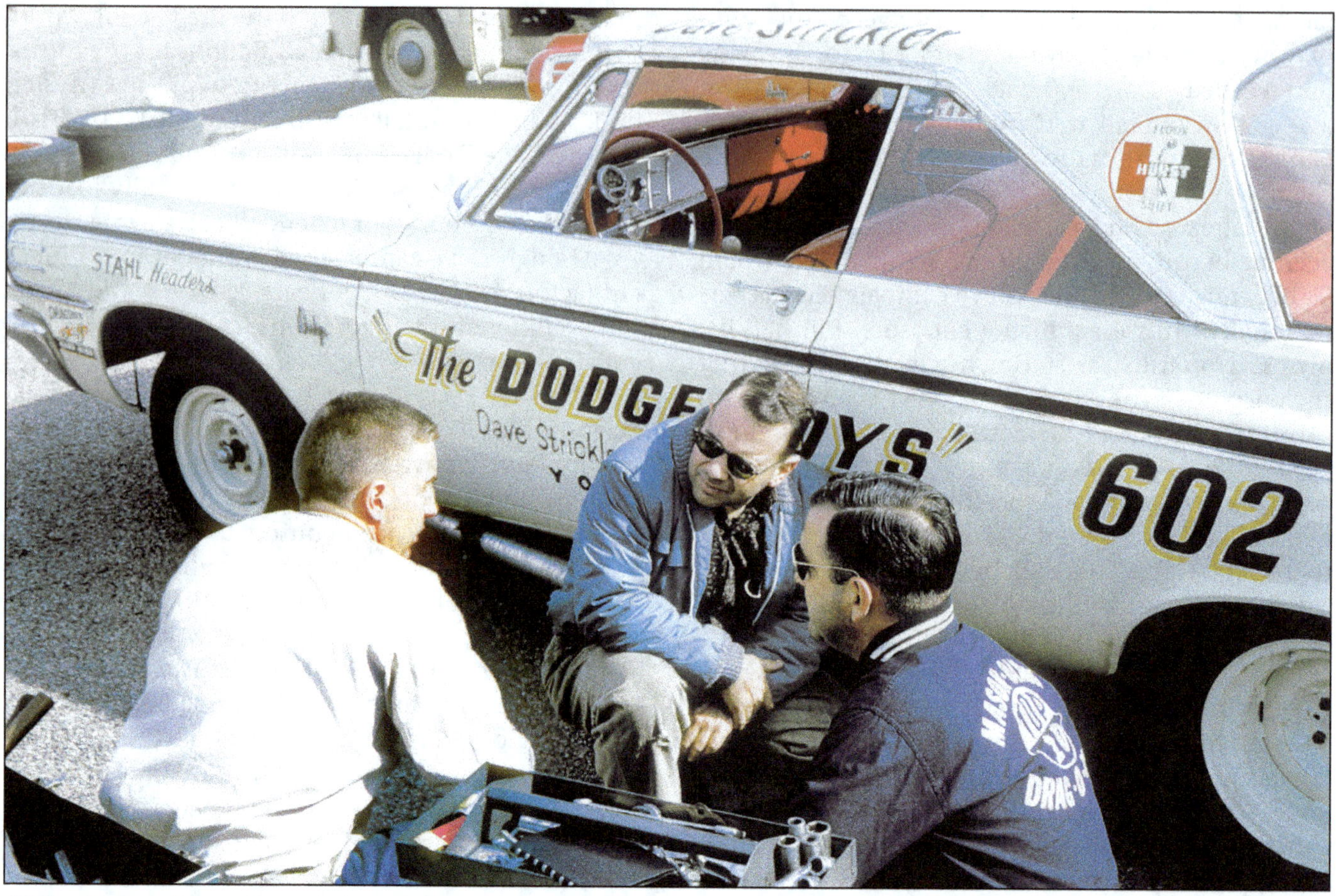

Chapter Three

At the Mason Dixon Drag-O-Way in Maryland, Strickler and Jenkins discuss concerns with a tech official. (Photo Courtesy Mike Strickler)

Chrysler factory deals were generous, and generally spared no expense to ensure a winning effort. Here, The Dodge Boys *Polara is seen during its West Coast trip to the AHRA and NHRA winter meets.* (Photo Courtesy Mike Strickler)

The Chrysler Years: 1964-1965

cars ready. Bill was not physically able to go 24 hours without sleep, so in the middle of the night he would crawl into the back seat of one of the cars and take a nap. I could go for 36 to 40 hours, as long as I had something to eat every four hours or so. Thankfully, there was a diner just down the road."

The trip west was not without incident. Leaving at about 10:30 pm, Bill drove Bud Faubel's underpowered 318 pickup, towing the *Honker* Dodge. Meanwhile, Jere crawled into the passenger seat beside him and caught up on his sleep. It wasn't long into the trip when Jere felt the tires leaving the road. It was sometime after 11:00 pm, in the middle of a freezing January evening, and Bill was pulling over to adjust the ignition timing! Mission accomplished, he pulled back on the road, and off they went. A short while later, Jere felt the truck leave the pavement again. Bill had pulled off the road to adjust the timing once more. To quote Jere: "This was all dictated by the dyno that was built into his ass."

Eventually, the pair met up with Dave Strickler and his entourage at a predetermined location on the Pennsylvania Turnpike. Bill decided that Bud's truck was so underpowered it would take him forever to get to California and took over driving Strickler's 426-powered truck. A broken motor mount slowed down the Strickler truck. This, in combination with Bill's refusal to drive faster than 50 mph on the country roads and 70 mph on the freeway, allowed them to arrive on the West Coast 4 or 5 hours after the Faubel truck. So much for taking the faster truck!

At the AHRA Winternationals (Beeline Dragway, Arizona), Strickler and Jenkins captured Super Stock honors with the new Dodge, defeating Hayden Proffitt with an 11.97 elapsed time. They weren't as fortunate at the NHRA winter meet; the team was eliminated in the first round by *Ford Thunderbolt* of Gas Ronda.

With the mid-season introduction of the legendary 426 Hemi engine, the Super Stock Polara was

The business card of The Dodge Boys, which even gives a home residence address! How times have changed. (Bill Jenkins Collection)

Bill and the Super Stock Dodge in Arizona for the AHRA Winternationals. It turned out to be a very worthwhile trip. (Photo Courtesy Mike Strickler)

Chapter Three

parked in favor of an altered-wheelbase car, which Strickler and Jenkins campaigned in NHRA Factory Experimental class. Before being sold to parts unknown, the Polara saw a garden-variety big-block swapped in place of the Max Wedge.

The altered-wheelbase car, referred to in most circles as a "2-percent" car, was one of the original four "altered" cars produced by Chrysler. These 2-percent cars were specially modified Dodges and Plymouths built specifically for drag racing. The wheelbase was shuffled forward by 2 percent of its total length, placing greater weight on the rear wheels for improved traction and improved quarter-mile times. Additional modifications to the cars included the thin-gauge fenders, hoods, and doors, the fiberglass bumpers, a plastic windshield and side glass, and an aluminum dashboard. Total weight for these cars was about 3,240 pounds.

The car was delivered with a 426 Hemi, though it was initially run using a Stage III 426 Max Wedge. Bill tweaked the Hemi and the drag racing world didn't see the new engine until mid May. The newly developed 426, with its twin big-gulping Carter carburetors, golf-ball-size valves, and superior hemispherical (Hemi) combustion chambers proceeded to dominate the world of drag racing, powering everything from old deuce coupes to Top Fuel dragsters.

By mid-season, Bill had *The Dodge Boys* Hemi humming. During a match race against the Dick Brannan Ford at Cecil County (once referred to as the Traction Capitol of the East), *The Dodge Boys* set the A/FX record with a 10.81-second run at 128.75 mph.

Without a dynamometer to hook the car up to, Bill was known to slip a pair of mufflers on the Dodge and take it for a late-night run down Route 30. A quick jaunt generally told him what he needed to know, and the car was back in the shop and the lights off before the police showed up. Apparently, the old woman who owned the building lived on a street behind the shop, and wasn't much of a fan of these late-night blasts.

Things were not all peaches and cream in the land of The Dodge Boys, though. As early as July there was talk of a forthcoming split. Dave had mentioned he had intentions of splitting with Bill and going his own way at the end of the season. Bill, who got wind of Dave's plans, was going to throw him

Bill and Dave accept a trophy for their 1964 AHRA Winternationals win. Though the pair had switched brands after the 1963 season, their winning ways continued. (Photo Courtesy Mike Strickler)

The Chrysler Years: 1964-1965

and his cars out immediately. He could threaten this because *The Dodge Boys* cars were usually kept in Berwyn at Bill's shop: Dave had no place to work on them in York. (With a change of decals, Bud Faubel did run *The Dodge Boys* 2-percent car.)

At the time, *The Dodge Boys* and Faubel's car needed work; neither was running up to par. Jere Stahl convinced Bill that he shouldn't quit while the cars' performance was down and suggested that he hire Tony Pizzi and Joe Tryson to work part time until the cars were ready. Both Tony and Joe had been customers of Bill's, and had spent time at the Sonoco because it was a local hangout. The decision was made, they were hired, and Bill split from Dave after the NHRA Nationals in September.

An interesting shot of the two Dodge Boys cars. The freshly painted A/FX car is on the trailer, and the Super Stock car is to the left. Note how the Super Stock car is minus "The Dodge Boys" lettering. (Photo Courtesy Mike Strickler)

Dave getting the jump on Don Nicholson at Cecil County. Though Factory Experimental rules may have been fairly lax, they did dictate that all cars be manufactured in the current year. Outside of the dominating 427-powered Mercury Comets of Don Nicholson and Ronnie Sox, there was little competition for these new altered Dodges and Plymouths. (Photo Courtesy John Durand)

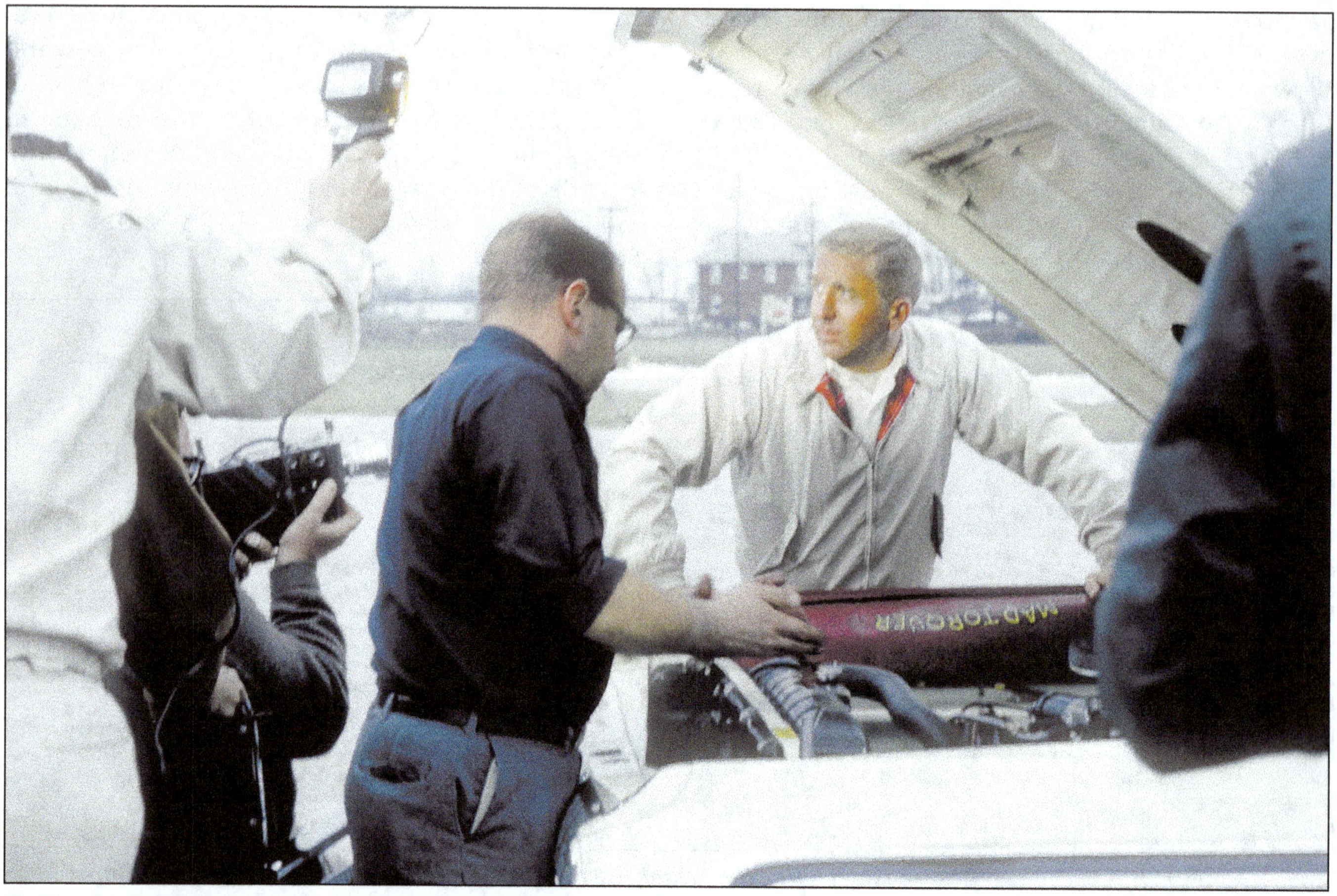

Chapter Three

By the mid 1960s, drag racing had shaken its bad-boy image and was appearing on national television shows, such as the Wide World of Sports*. Here,* The Dodge Boys *give a rare television interview, featuring their Super Stock Polara.* (Photo Courtesy Mike Strickler)

You can't help noticing the length of the tuned exhaust collectors. Different lengths were tried until the optimal size, based on improved ETs, was determined. The adjustable traction arm for the rear suspension is barely visible. (Photo Courtesy Mike Strickler)

The Chrysler Years: 1964–1965

Jenkins Competition, as it was now known, employed Joe Tryson for the next 30 years, minus a couple years given up to Uncle Sam. Tony opened his own performance shop in 1966.

A caravan of Jenkins-tuned cars that included Strickler, Faubel, and Joe Gardner's *Northwind* headed for Indiana in September, seeking gold at the Nationals. The Dodge Boys were the only lucky ones this day, capturing the A/FX crown by defeating Tom Grove's *Melrose Missile* in the final go, with an easy 11.04-second pass.

Chrysler, wanting to be sure they were well represented in Super Stock at the Nationals, provided Dave Strickler with a specially prepared, S/SA Hemi Dodge. The car wouldn't make much of a showing, holding down the number-6 qualifying position with

Yet to be painted and prepared, here's the NHRA Nationals' only Super Stock car. This Hemi-powered, automatic transmission-equipped Dodge was sold not long after the race. (Photo Courtesy Mike Strickler)

The SS/A car in action at the NHRA Nationals. Dave qualified this and the A/FX car, while Bill ensured the Hemi's performance was up to par. (Photo Courtesy John Durand)

Chapter Three

an 11.61. Bob Harropp put away the Super Stock car in the first round with an 11.66 to Dave's 11.33 (foul start). Bud Faubel, in his *Honker* Dodge, made it as far as the stock semifinals before being eliminated. Joe Gardner? Well, he made plans to race elsewhere. During the Nationals, the NHRA approached Strickler and Jenkins to ask if they'd be interested in joining the growing list of drag racers heading to England as part of the United States Drag Racing Team. Bill, wanting to make the trip, made the decision at that time to finish out the season with Dave.

In mid September, the pair joined fellow racers Don Garlits, Tommy Ivo, Tony Nancy, K. S. Pitman, Ronnie Sox, George Montgomery, and others,

As the flag starter runs, Dave Strickler makes another easy launch in **The Dodge Boys** *(the A/FX Hemi-powered Mopar) during the 1964 USA Drag Team tour of England. Since no domestic European product could have kept up with the latest drag technology from the United States, his opponent at these events was Ronnie Sox in the Sox & Martin Mercury Comet.* (Photo Courtesy Lynn Wineland Archive/www.quartermilestones.com)

The Dodge Boys share a laugh while topping the tank with some Go-Go juice for the Hemi. The A/FX Dodge, which had thrilled the English crowds, was sold shortly after returning home. (Lynn Wineland Archive/www.quartermilestones.com)

The Chrysler Years: 1964-1965

aboard the USS *United States* for a six-week trip to merry old England.

The Dodge Boys' main competitor on the trip was Ronnie Sox's 427 Comet. Between them, they divided wins at the six venues the touring group visited. All ETs turned for the pair, on the less-than-perfect airstrips on which they ran, were off-pace mid-to-high 11-second times.

Bill remembered the trip as a nice vacation. The most memorable moments for him included taking in the museums and driving on the opposite side of the road through the heart of London.

Upon his return from England (and after a lengthy courtship), Dave married Ammon Smith's granddaughter. The couple remained happily married until Dave's passing in June 1985.

Strickler and Jenkins parted ways on a high note. In mid November, they captured both ends of the Factory Experimental record during a season-ending match at Cecil County. *Drag News* reported on the pair's defeat of Buddy Martin, who was wheeling the Sox & Martin Comet. Strickler turned a 10.65 at 131.92 mph.

Bill's BDRA membership card—a must-have for the English drag racer. (Bill Jenkins Collection)

A rare photo of Dave Strickler, Bill Jenkins, and the 2-percent A/FX car in England. Part of tuning for track conditions could include swapping the transmission, rear end, and rear springs back and forth as a group. (Photo Courtesy Mike Strickler)

Chapter Three

During the same month, the now-defunct *Super Stock & Drag Illustrated* magazine appeared on the newsstands for the first time. As if he didn't have enough on his plate already, Bill agreed to take on the position of technical advisor. His key responsibility was to answer the monthly technical questions sent in by the readers and chosen by the editor to appear in the next issue. The upside for Bill was the free publicity garnered. Bill held this position until 1968.

What became of The Dodge Boys' cars? The Super Stock Max Wedge car was last reported to be owned by Jim Kramer of Pittsburgh, and has apparently spent its life as a race car. The 2-percent Factory Experimental car was sold immediately after returning from England to George Whalen and continued to run A/FX through 1965. Today the car is owned by collector Mike Guffey.

The Super Stock Hemi car is unrestored, and has spent its life as a race car running as quick as 9.50. Frank Lupo of Dynamic Transmissions has owned the car since 1965, and he parked it in 1991 because "it just became too valuable to race."

Bud Faubel's Honkin' Dodges

Bud Faubel was instrumental in The Dodge Boys' deal and was introduced to Bill by Dave Strickler in 1961. This is how Bud came to have Bill perform some tuning on his 1964 Dodge late in 1963. NASCAR legend Marvin Paunch witnessed how fast Bud's cars were, and he had suggested the name—*Honker* because the car really flew.

With Bill turning the wrenches for Bud full time in 1964, Bud set a new S/SA-class record at Cecil County while downing Bill Lawton's Ford *Thunderbolt*. With Bill's help, Bud saw the Stage III 426 Max Wedge–powered *Honker* go from 12.20-second times down to a record-setting 11.39.

A stickler for detail, Jenkins balanced and blueprinted the 426 and fine-tuned at the track. In a *Cars* magazine article dated 1964, Bill stated that there was no real magic to what he was doing—just plain common sense and a strict attention to detail. Bill's raceday tool chest included a portable weather station capable of reading atmospheric pressure and humidity. Weather conditions are important for obvious

Bud Faubel, having run one in the very early 1960s, was the first drag racer to find success using the TorqueFlite automatic transmission. Chrysler also supplied Bud with the first TorqueFlite-equipped Hemi-powered car. (Photo Courtesy Mike Strickler)

The Chrysler Years: 1964-1965

reasons, but few paid much attention to them the way Bill did. In true engineering practice, he maintained an accurate record of all changes made and the effect the changes had on a specific run.

Another tool Bill also habitually carried, starting in the 1950s, was his trusty slide rule. It came in handy for calculating compression ratio, lift, and tire size.

Bud's second 1964 car was Hemi-powered, and again prepared by Jenkins. This car was a factory-lightweight 330 sedan, incorporating the first automatic transmission behind a Hemi. Horsepower approached 600, allowing the car to run an S/SA record-holding time of 11.04 seconds at 125.52 mph. At the NHRA Nationals, Bud and *Hemi Honker* turned 11.74 while losing in the semifinals to Jim Thorton's Rancharger Dodge. Faubel's car was eventually modified to run A/FX and was match-raced, producing times in the 10.80-second range.

Faubel amassed 200-plus wins in 1964. At the end of the year he was voted the York US-30 Driver of the Year, thanks in large part to Bill Jenkins tuning skills.

Bud's career wound down after campaigning a fiberglass Dodge Dart with George Weiler. He was also a commercial airline pilot, and scheduling conflicts eventually forced his early retirement from the sport.

Today, Bud's schedule includes ballroom dancing, taking in the occasional drag race reunion, and showing up every day at the dealership he still operates in his hometown of Chambersburg. Now close to 80 years of age, Bud is finally considering retirement.

Black Arrow Plymouth, 1965

The drag racing career of Robert "Doc" Burgess began in 1963 behind the wheel of a Chevy Corvair that he ran (for kicks) at New York's Dover Dragstrip. Doc enjoyed the sport and developed a need for speed. The following year he invested in a 426-powered Plymouth. The car ran AS/A and won 29 out of 32 starts on local tracks. Doc noted, "We installed a set of headers on the car and went drag racing. This was the extent of my mechanical experience."

When Doc caught wind of Chrysler's forthcoming Super Stock Hemi-powered car, he decided to step things up and make the investment. Knowing that he lacked the knowledge to build a winning combination, he sought the help of Bill Jenkins. He said, "We had no real drag racing experience, but knew enough that we had better go to someone who could give us the best help and the best car."

The final go at the NHRA Winternationals saw Bill reading the tree to perfection. The hole-shot lead proved to be too much for Dick Housey to make up. (Photo Courtesy John Durand)

Chapter Three

Doc purchased the Plymouth through Bud Faubel at Coldbrook Motors in Chambersburg, Pennsylvania. Bill made arrangements to prepare the car for quarter-mile action and, in exchange, Bill ran the car at the NHRA Winternationals with his own name on the sides. In retrospect, Doc Burgess said, "I should have made sure I was listed as the owner of the car and that my name was on it."

Though ordered through Bud Faubel's dealership, Doc recalls Bill picking the car up directly from Chrysler. He was pressed for time and wanted to be sure the car was ready for a Winternationals debut. Doc didn't have a name in mind, so the Plymouth was christened *Black Arrow*, after a sailboat Bill's parents had owned.

Summer student employee Frank Hurley had pinned the "Grumpy" nickname on Bill back in 1962 due to his no-nonsense, down-to-business work ethic, and *Black Arrow* was the first car to carry the moniker. The name, which seemed appropriate then just as it does now, has stuck with him to this day.

Black Arrow was one of Chrysler's rare "A990" cars, as they have come to be known. These cars were picked off the assembly line by Chrysler engineers and assembled specifically for drag racing. The A990 designation refers to the specially built Hemi engines powering these cars. But, over time, enthusiasts attached the name to the complete package.

Upgrades to the base Hemi included aluminum cylinder heads, a high-lift camshaft, a magnesium intake manifold (with a pair of Holley 4-barrel carburetors), and tubular headers. Horsepower for these beasts was estimated to be about 550.

Admitting the car was not running up to par, Jenkins relied on some fine driving to win his first national event. (Chrysler Corporation/Bill Jenkins Collection)

The Chrysler Years: 1964–1965

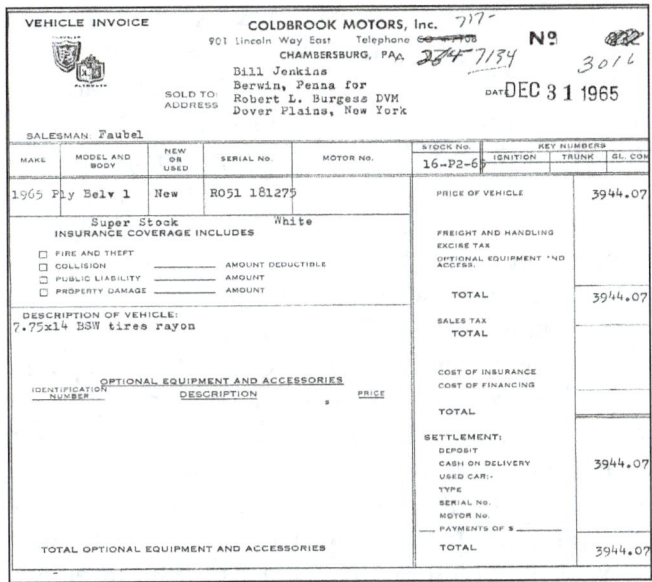

There has always been some confusion over who actually owned Black Arrow, and this dates back to the Winternationals of 1965 when Doc's name was not on the car. Hopefully, the original bill of sale eliminates any doubt. (Photo Courtesy Robert Burgess)

Factory modifications included lightweight bucket seats and thinner-gauge metal fenders, hoods, doors, bumpers, and radiator supports. Side and rear glass was cut from lightweight Chemcor; with the rear quarter windows in a fixed position, no operating mechanisms were ever installed. The hood was held on with fasteners and there was no use for weight-adding items such as the heater, radio, rear seat, armrests, or carpet padding. Even the right-side sun visor and dome light were excluded.

Though the 4-speed transmission was available, *Black Arrow* was equipped with the heavy-duty TorqueFlite automatic transmission. It had an 8¾-inch rear end carrying 4.56:1 gears. The special leaf springs shortened the wheelbase 1 inch by moving the rear housing forward. To aid weight transfer, the cars were equipped with a 95-pound truck battery, which was mounted in the trunk.

Drag News reported on *Black Arrow's* debut on January 3, running S/SA at Cecil County. In what must have been a surprise to many, Bill was now competing against his old partner Dave Strickler, who started the season running last year's *The Dodge Boys* S/SA car. Throughout the meet, Jenkins and Strickler banged off 11-teens and came face to face in the Top Stock Eliminator final. Both cars were running 9-inch slicks and pulled to the line together for the final go. As the last yellow bulb flashed to

By late spring, Doc Burgess was briefly partnered with Carl Spiedel in campaigning Black Arrow. Bill shared in the driving chores through the fall, but didn't like the modified wheelbase. (Photo Courtesy Mike Spiedel)

The 1965 A990-code Plymouth Black Arrow truly heralded Jenkins' introduction to the drag racing world as a driver. Prior to this, he was primarily noted as a premier tuner and engine builder. Jenkins defeated Dick Housey (in a nearly identical car) for the title at Pomona. (Lynn Wineland Archive/www.quartermilestones.com)

Grumpy's Toys

Chapter Three

green, the two cars were gone, side by side through first gear. Dave lost his TorqueFlite transmission at second gear, handing the win to Grumpy, who tripped the lights with a remarkable 10.95-second pass at 131 mph!

At the end of January, Bill took leave of his "Tech Corner" responsibilities at *Super Stock & Drag Illustrated,* locked the doors of Jenkins Competition, and headed west for the AHRA and NHRA Winternationals.

The first stop for the new car was the AHRA meet at Beeline Raceway in Arizona. Jenkins didn't fare too well here. He bowed out in the first round (with engine troubles) to eventual winner Roger Lindamood in the *Color Me Gone* Dodge. Referring to the loss, Bill said he had been trying a new set of pistons and "just couldn't get the car set up and running right."

Then, it was on to Pomona, California, and the NHRA Winternationals, where Bill hoped the bugs could be worked out. Though the car was still running rough, Pomona was good to Bill. He recorded his first-ever NHRA National event victory, capturing S/SA honors and taking Top Stock Eliminator.

Bill defeated Dick Housey's factory-backed Plymouth in the final go with an 11.39-second run at 126.05 mph to Dick's quicker (but losing) 11.37-second pass at 126.76 mph. Through each round of Winternationals eliminations, Bill got the jump on each of his opponents, winning the race on the starting line. This was his first and only National-event win in a non-Chevrolet product.

Beating the factory-backed teams at the Winternationals was a win that Bill savored for some time. Having proven to be more than capable behind the wheel, he met with Chrysler representative Bob Cahill after he returned from the West Coast. He hoped to work out a factory deal of his own, but it didn't happen. Bob recalled, "Our deals were all made for the season by then." There was no way they could consider signing Bill after the Winternationals.

In March 1965, Doc and *Black Arrow* defeated Tom Snedon's *Bounty Hunter* Dodge three straight times during a match race session at Dover Dragstrip in New York. In the process, the car produced a quick 10.71-second elapsed time. By this point in the season, the keys to *Black Arrow* had been handed back

Bill made arrangements with Doc Burgess to run the car at the winter meets, in hopes of gaining a factory deal. The first major outing for the Arrow was the AHRA Winternationals, where Grumpy bowed out early due to mechanical issues. (Photo Courtesy John Durand)

The Chrysler Years: 1964–1965

Bill Jenkins earned permanent acclaim in the Mopar world by beating a stout group of competitors to win Top Stock Eliminator honors at the 1965 NHRA Winternationals. In this rare image, he is parading in front of the crowd with the winner's flag, a special creation by NHRA. As part of his winnings, Hurst rewarded him with a weeklong Hawaiian vacation. (Lynn Wineland Archive/www.quartermilestones.com)

Living just 5 miles from New York's Dover Dragstrip, Doc called this his home away from home. More than capable behind the wheel, Doc captured numerous track records in Super Stock, Modified Production, and later Factory Experimental. (Robert Burgess Collection)

Chapter Three

to owner Doc Burgess, who went on to successfully campaign the car, however briefly, in conjunction with Bill Spidel. Doc noted that he continued to run Jenkins' engine, but Spidel failed to contribute and the partnership ended rather quickly.

In the June 1965 issue of *Super Stock & Drag Illustrated*, Bill stated how, with a little more tuning, *Black Arrow* could have pulled NHRA-legal 10-second times, and he was right. *Black Arrow* went on to run a 10.99 at Cecil County on 7-inch slicks. This has been reported to be the first 10-second elapsed time turned by a legal NHRA Stock-class car.

In order to better "plant" *Black Arrow* on its 7-inch slicks, suspension modifications included the Jenkins-built adjustable pinion snubber and shimming the front leaf-spring supports to help compensate for spring wind-up. This wind-up phenomenon is caused when the pinion gear tries to climb the ring gear, and is common in leaf-sprung cars. They also used unequal-length rear shackles to help equalize chassis loading when coming off the starting line. Those fortunate to have watched the car in action claimed nothing else launched quite like it.

Bill switched classes later in the year, at the NHRA Nationals in Indianapolis. He climbed behind the wheel again and shot *Black Arrow* to the A/MP class win with an 11.11-second elapsed time. He again bested Dick Housey, who lost the race on the line by catching the dreaded red light. Bill, who had driven *Arrow* to a quick 10.95 during street eliminations, eventually lost to Charlie Allen's Dodge. By the end of 1965, *Black Arrow* had gained injector stacks, an altered wheelbase, and was running NHRA Factory Experimental. The rear wheel wells were stretched by a local blacksmith and the rear suspension was made adjustable. A simple adjustment allowed the car to be returned to a stock wheelbase and run Super Stock.

That November, Bill made his final appearance in the car, winning the 2,800-pound class at the Super Stock Nationals held in Richmond, Virginia. Sporting fuel injectors and the shorter (100-inch) altered wheelbase, Bill knocked off a quick 10.44-second run at 125.61 mph.

Doc sold *Arrow* in 1968 and the new owner renamed it *Storm King* and ran the car in NHRA's

In its final form at the Super Stock Nationals in 1966, Black Arrow *weighed 2,600 pounds and ran high-9-second quarter-mile times with an injected Hemi on a 100-inch wheelbase. Doc ran the car successfully through 1967, alternating between the stock 115-inch wheelbase and the short 100-inch setup.* (Robert Burgess Collection)

The Chrysler Years: 1964-1965

A/XS (Experimental Stock) and C/Altered classes. Eventually, the abused hulk was stripped and the usable parts installed on a Super Stock car. The remains of *Black Arrow* were scrapped.

In the spring of 1965, Chevrolet unleashed its 396-ci Mark IV big-block. The engine was an outgrowth of the Mark II mystery motor that shook the troops at Daytona in 1963. "Semi Hemi" was one of the names used to describe the unique canted-valve layout that helped the engine to produce upwards of 425 hp. Bill's first experience with the new engine came from behind the wheel of a customer's Corvette. When he took the car out for a test drive after a major tune, Bill blew the rear end while pulling second gear and limped back to the shop, hoping the wheels didn't fall off. The Corvette was returned to the dealership, where the rear end was repaired under warranty.

In 1965, Jenkins Competition was responsible for more than 30 national records. Stock and Super Stock royalty such as Jack Werst, Joe Delorenzo, and Bill Spanako each carried Bill Jenkins' name into the winner's circle. Ironically, most of the Jenkins Competition–prepared cars in the winner's circle were lower Stock-class Chevrolets, while Bill drove a Plymouth and pursued a Chrysler sponsorship deal.

Jenkins Competition employee Tony Pizzi partnered with Philadelphia resident Carlo "Ollie" Volpe in campaigning a Jenkins-prepared A/SP 1965 Corvette. Ollie's Corvette was powered by a 375-hp fuel-injected 327-ci small-block, and played a key role in Bill's move from Chrysler back to Chevrolets.

Ollie approached Bill while looking to transform his street-driven Corvette into a full-time race car, and Bill obliged. To help offset the costs of having Jenkins build the car, Ollie did odd jobs around the Berwyn shop.

Through connections in the Sun Oil Company fuel lab (at Marcus Hook, Pennsylvania), Bill was able to make use of the in-house dynamometer. This was his first use of a dyno and he took full advantage of it, using Ollie's Corvette to test different fuels and headers, and even swapping out the fuel injection system for a carburetor and high-rise manifold. Bill knew a 350-hp carbureted version of the L-84 would be an option in the lightweight Chevy II in 1966 and, based on his time on the dyno, he felt the combination could be competitive. The Corvette's horsepower peaked at 425 and, when Tony wasn't snapping rear axle half-shafts, the car could run 11.15-second passes on an 11.80-second class record.

Bill quit the mom-and-pop side of his tune-up business for good in 1965, and concentrated on drag racing full-time. His main focus was prepping Chevrolet and Chrysler products, but he was also known to pull some good power from the occasional Oldsmobile, Pontiac, and Ford. Don't expect to find any photos of a Ford with Jenkins Competition decals pasted on the sides though; not everyone received a pair.

Monster Mash Chevy: The Original Grumpy's Toy?

Excluding his own cars, the *Monster Mash* Chevys of Andy and Bill Spanakos were probably the most notable cars to fly the Jenkins banner. Rumors of the final demise of *Monster Mash* cars have swirled for years. The one that seems to have gained the most notoriety has one of the cars (there were two of them) being crushed to hide the speed secrets of Bill Jenkins. It's made for some great folklore, but read on.

Bill "Spider" Spanakos first approached Jenkins in the summer of 1960 with a two-tone, green-and-white four-door 1955 Chevy Bel Air. Short on funds, Spider offered to work in Jenkins' shop in exchange for work done on the car. Bill, always the big softy, agreed to the proposition and initially put Spider to work cleaning parts. Spider continued to work for Jenkins on and off through 1966.

The four-door, which weighed 3,200, fell into NHRA's I/Stock category. But, being on the heavier end of the class weight break, successes were minimal. In mid 1960, the car was sold and replaced by

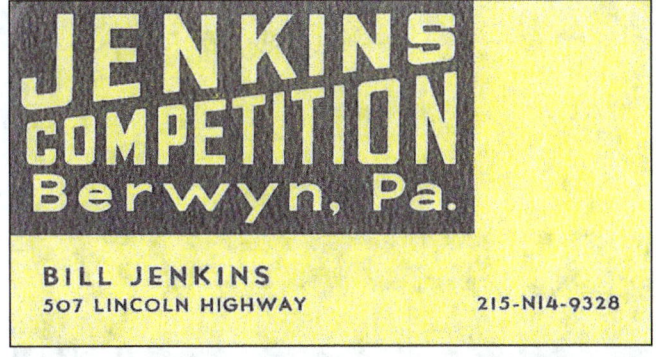

A rare Jenkins Competition business card from when Bill worked out of the old Sonoco station in Berwyn, Pennsylvania. The Sonoco is long gone but the logo remains. To this day, Bill uses this design on all his letterheads. (Bill Jenkins Collection)

Chapter Three

a lighter and more-desirable 1955 Chevy Two-Ten two-door. This first *Monster Mash* gained both the Spanakos brothers and Jenkins national recognition in 1963. It set the NHRA I/Stock national record at a shade over 94 mph. Further recognition came in February 1965, when *Super Stock & Drag Illustrated* published a feature article on the car. By the time the article appeared, the car had been replaced. Better late notoriety than none!

Monster Mash ran as quick as 14.13-seconds at 96.60 mph before being sold to John Martini of Canton, Ohio. To this day *Monster Mash* survives in 1980s-era street trim and resides in Florida.

Monster Mash II could be described as the ultimate Junior Stocker. The old Bell Telephone car was campaigned from mid 1963 through 1966 by the Spanakos brothers, and drew nearly as much attention to Bill and his tuning capabilities as the previous *Old Reliable* cars had. *Monster Mash II* was a lighter One-Fifty utility sedan. It weighed 3,055 pounds, placing the car at the more favorable end of NHRA's I/Stock. Powered by a 0.060-inch overbored 265-ci V-8, the car won its class at Indy in 1964 and later set the class record at Cecil County with an astounding 13.34-second run at 103.50 mph. Spider and *Monster Mash II* won the Division One points championship in both 1965 and 1966.

With Bill's guidance, Spider eventually assembled his own engines and relied on Bill's supervision and tuning skills to get the most out of them. The Stock-class rules were not as liberal as they are today; engine modifications to the *Mash* car were limited. They were going to use Forgedtrue replacement pistons, but, after burning holes in a few during a record attempt at York, they decided to build a fresh engine, making use of cast slugs.

Jenkins/Spanakos started with a 1956 265-ci block (rather than a 1955) because of its better oiling and superior casting. They bored it to .060 inch over stock, producing 274 ci. The cylinders were filled with garden-variety cast replacement pistons. Bill knew cast pistons actually performed better and you could make more power with them, if you could make them last. They used a set of NHRA-approved "service" heads in place of the original units. While outwardly appearing identical to the 265 heads, the replacements proved to have valve pockets with superior flow characteristics. They milled down the head's deck surfaces, bringing the combustion chamber sizes down to the NHRA legal minimum volume, and the pistons were notched for valve clearance. Final compression was approximately 10:1.

The greatest power gain came with the installation of a blueprinted camshaft, which started out as a blank core. Jenkins says of the cam, "Chevrolet's own 195-hp 'service' camshaft would not meet their own specifications by a considerable amount, so we took the specifications given to the NHRA and made

Bill and Andy Spanakos terrorized the East Coast stocker ranks with their pair of Monster Mash Chevys. Jenkins referred to these as his "house cars" due to the attention lavished on them. The first Monster Mash car is seen here at York, Pennsylvania, circa 1964. (Photo Courtesy John Durand)

The Chrysler Years: 1964-1965

camshafts to those specs." The ramp speed was modified and the cam may go from 112 to 108 to 110 degrees of lobe separation. The spent gases exited through a pair of Stahl headers. By Jenkins' own estimate, the little 265 was producing in the neighborhood of 350 to 370 hp.

Backing the 265 was a "slick shift" Saginaw 3-speed transmission that Spider claimed was good for up to 90 runs. The first use of this treatment was in Jenkins employee Tony Pizzi's record-setting C/Stock 409-powered 1962 Bel Air (with its Borg-Warner T-10 4-speed transmission). Unbeknown to Bill at the time, Chrysler engineers were designing their own version of the slick shift transmission. As described by Bill, "The clutch collar and clutch hub is where you started, and then the teeth on the syncro sleeve were turned down 1/4 inch, along with every second tooth on the corresponding dog gear. On later transmissions, every second tooth was ground off completely. We'd take the whole gear stack up in the transmission, allowing optimal location as far as gear mesh was concerned."

Bill personally prepared the transmissions for both *Monster Mash II* and Joe Cox's *Hostage* 1955 Chevy wagon, before demands on his time forced him to pass the work off. Transmission specialist Alex Jarrell was the recipient of Bill's generosity.

Additional modifications to *Monster Mash II* included acid-dipped bumpers and brackets, along with "possibly other body parts." The loose front shocks were added along with 1958 Chevrolet spindles and modified A-arms were incorporated as a way to improve front-end lift and geometry. Out back, traction links and new, stiffer shocks were the only modifications.

Few people could interpret the rule book the way that Bill Jenkins did. Issues such as frame alignment (or misalignment) and engine positioning were questioned by the NHRA tech inspectors during the 1965 Nationals. Prepared plausible excuses, such as "a bent frame that had previously gone undetected" were offered. Another example: The car had a horn, but it was inoperable since the underside of the dashboard and the steering column had been

In 1964, the Borg-Warner 4-speed transmission in Tony Pizzi's A/S 409-powered Bel Air was the first to use Jenkins' "slick shift" treatment. (Photo Courtesy Jim Pizzi)

Chapter Three

stripped of all but the essentials. When the NHRA Tech Inspector asked Spider to blow the horn, he reached in the window, pressed the button, and said "beep." In not so many words, the tech inspector said, "You can't do that." Bill Jenkins jumped in and quoted straight from the rule book, "...must have a horn." The rules didn't say anything about it working. The man had an answer for everything that day.

Monster Mash II ran J/Stock at the NHRA Springnationals in 1966 and took class win with a 14.16-second run at 96.87 mph. It was not long afterward that the car was sold to Dink Lawrence, who painted the car red and campaigned it for a couple of seasons in conjunction with Jenkins employee Pete Preston. Neither was very successful at operating the venerable 3-speed transmission, and it wasn't long before the three transmissions that Spider had sold with the car were worn out. Spider built one useable transmission out of the three and then proceeded to run a 13.90-second pass with the car. The new owner had problems going any quicker than a mid-14. Neither Dink nor Pete ever really got a handle on the 3-speed. They replaced it with a Powerglide 2-speed automatic, and it ran slower. The car eventually ended up in the hands of a couple gents from Hackettstown, New Jersey. During a trek down Route 87 in New York, the trailer (with the car onboard) came unhooked from the tow vehicle and careened off a hillside. The car was wrecked beyond repair and, sadly, this was the pitiful end of one of the most famous stockers in drag racing history.

What of Bill "Spider" Spanakos? In 2008, at 68 years of age, Spider was recognized by the NHRA as the longest-participating drag racer. He's been at it for 53 years and currently runs a P/SA 1965 Chevelle station wagon, which set class records in 1998 through 2005. To quote Spider: "As long as I can get in a car, I'll be driving."

As for the origins of the nickname "Spider": At one time Spanakos worked with spider monkeys at the veteran's hospital in Coatesville, Pennsylvania.

Monster Mash *as she sits today, powered by a tunnel-rammed 350-ci V-8. Will the owner restore the car back to its former status? Only he knows for certain.* (Photo Courtesy Chris Ciccarone)

The Chrysler Years: 1964–1965

Dink Lawrence and Pete Preston campaigned this Jenkins-prepped SS/EA Yenko Camaro into the 1971 season. Pete noted, that it was "no fault of the car, but it never ran up to expectations and showed little success." This was one of three Yenko Camaros specifically built for drag racing in 1969, and the only one remaining today. The Camaro was auctioned in 2009 for $297,000. (Photo Courtesy Carl Rubrecht)

Here's a look at Monster Mash's stablemate, Joe Cox's record-setting 1955 Chevrolet wagon. Doug Mentzer carried on the car's winning ways after buying it in 1968. (Photo Courtesy Carl Rubrecht)

The best remembered match-ups in NHRA's Stock categories in 1966 were the A/S battles between Bill Jenkins and Jere Stahl. Seen here at Indy, the Chevy II lost out to Stahl's Belvedere in the final round. (Photo Courtesy Ray Mann Collection www.quartermilestones.com)

Chapter Four

Super Stockers: 1966–1969

For no reason other than to prove a point, Bill made the decision to build and drive his own cars starting in 1966. To him, the stockers were the only game in town. He built his reputation and business upon them, and he could never really imagine himself behind the wheel of anything else.

Grumpy's Toy I, 1966 Chevy II

Due to Bill's inability to gain a Chrysler sponsorship deal of his own, he returned to the Chevrolet camp in 1966. A Regal Red L-79 327 (350 hp) Chevy II was purchased from Ammon R. Smith. Bill armed it with the knowledge he gained from the time spent with Carlo Volpe's Corvette. The little Chevy II was readied to do battle come February

With a weight-to-horsepower factor of approximately 8 pounds per hp, the car fell squarely into NHRA's A/Stock, a class that was dominated by Chrysler's street Hemis. Bill felt the car could be competitive there and, to the surprise of many, the Chevy II proved to be a winner, defeating most comers. The one thorn in Bill's side was the Hemi Belvedere campaigned by Jere Stahl. Bill hadn't counted on Jere building a Top Stocker in 1966, and it caught him by surprise.

Jere, who had no intentions of running an A/Stock car in 1966, changed his mind after building the headers for and driving *Super Stock & Drag Illustrated* magazine's Hemi-powered test car. Because he had so much fun with the car, he contacted Dick Maxwell of Chrysler's racing program and he proposed that, if he were to buy the car himself, they could give him a parts deal. Obviously a deal was struck and Jere went racing.

Though "Grumpy's Toy" had initially been painted on the car, as a good gimmick, the slogan seemed appropriate in 1966. Bill was frustrated at having to play runner-up at three of the four NHRA national events. All three losses were to Jere Stahl. To rub salt in the wound, the pair match raced numerous times throughout the season, with Jere's Belvedere winning more times than not.

"We knew if we beat Bill one week, we better be prepared because he would be coming back the next time with more horsepower," Jere recalled. Whether a three- or five-race match, the pair tried to please the fans by running every round. Appearance money for these match races ranged from $1,000 to $2,000 per show.

The 327, as prepared by Jenkins, was putting out an estimated 420 hp and he was making use of every last one of them. The car consistently turned mid-11-second ETs and share the national record with Jere Stahl with an 11.66-second time.

As described in a *Super Stock & Drag Illustrated* magazine article, Bill started with a .030-inch overbore of the 327. He then stuffed it with Forgedtrue replacement pistons outfitted with Dykes-design rings. The heads were milled to allowable minimum chamber volume, bringing the compression up to 11.6:1. Though cylinder head modifications were limited, Bill was sure to at least start with a good set. The "461"-numbered castings were preferred; they proved to have slightly more port volume. Bill explains: "There were two distinct volumes out of the 461 casting, and the ones ending with suffix 'X' had 6 to 8 more cc. Some of the non-X heads were also larger, so you had to check the heads to be sure." The story of Bill purchasing 24 cylinder heads, and returning 20 of them due to the fact they were of lesser volume, has circulated for years.

The valvetrain consisted of an Isky 550 flat-tappet camshaft with a 108-degree centerline and Crane roller rockers. An Edelbrock high-rise manifold was topped by a specially modified Holley 585-cfm carburetor. Numerous factors would determine jet choice and they would be swapped as required. The needle-and-seat assembly, along with power restrictions, was enlarged, increasing fuel flow. A stock single-point distributor running 39 degrees of total ignition advance received its power through a Prestolite transistor, and would fire the Champion plugs through Autolite wires. Exhaust initially exited through a set of Stahl four-tube headers, designed to Bill's own specifications. Bill later switched to a pair

Bruce Tucker recalls many dreadful hours peeling factory sealant from every nook and cranny of this car over the winter of 1965–1966. The red stripes on the roof were a jab at the Ramchargers who Bill took extra pleasure in beating. Overnight, Jenkins' Division 1 disciples followed suit. (Robert Snayko Photo, Courtesy of Jere Stahl Collection)

of Doug Thorley's Tri-Y headers; it was felt the primary length of the Stahl headers was too long. When Jenkins built his second Chevy II, he made the switch to Hooker Headers, his first paying sponsor.

To row the gears in the M-21 Muncie 4-speed manual transmission, Bill had created a shifter of his own design. He used a Hurst 3-speed shifter to move the four forward gears, with a separate lever for reverse. To actuate reverse, the 3-speed shifter was placed in the neutral position and the reverse lever pulled. This setup helped prevent the shifter from hanging up between gear changes. It had only one gate to travel through (as opposed to the standard 4-speed shifter, which had two). Consider this an early form of a vertical gate shifter with a reverse lockout, which was not available to consumers for a couple more years.

To get the Chevy II to launch and hook at 6,000-plus rpm on the 7-inch-wide tires, Bill took Jere Stahl's idea and ran soft compound M&H slicks at 7 to 12 pounds of air pressure, thus creating a larger footprint and gaining more traction. As Jere recalled, "I walked over to Bill's car after a WCS meet at Sanford, Maine, in June and let air out of his tires. Then I told him to either drive the way I'm going to explain or I'd drive it and show him. From that day on, there was no beating him by truck lengths again."

Jere admits that Dave Strickler told him what to do the previous year when he saw him struggling with low-pressure tires on his Junior Stock 1957 Chevy. "It was a day we were both at the York Airport breaking in engines the week before Indy in 1965. It took five rounds to win D/Stock that year, and every one of my opponents had pulled a red light and I was still ahead of them at the Christmas tree. The 1957 had something like 7 inches of travel in the front end, a 2.36:1 first gear transmission, Henry's axles, and [a] beefed-up rear end. I was making 7,000-rpm banzai starts like an A/FXer. It demoralized most of my opponents! Those guys didn't dare to really clean their tires for fear of breaking something in the drive line."

Jere also said, "I didn't do the tire pressure thing to Bill's Chevy II as a way of helping a competitor; I did it because I had no competition in A/S. I also owed Bill because I had learned so much from him in 1963 to 1964."

To further help the car hook, Bill devised his own set of traction bars and added more leaf springs. He added an extra shock absorber to the rear of the left leaf, because the spring had a tendency of deflecting away from the frame during initial acceleration. The 4.88:1 rear gears were annealed to a C55 rating to help prevent breakage. Bill had discovered, a long time back, that most gears were too brittle as

The L-79 Chevy II was more than just a gimmick and surprised many big-block Fords and Chryslers. Note the brackets hanging in the front—remains from the recently removed air dam. (Photo Courtesy David Smith)

Super Stockers: 1966–1969

supplied by the manufacturer. This caused them to break easily. To the best of Bill's recollection, this is the first of his innovations that General Motors put in its parts book.

Though General Motors had a strict "no racing" policy in place, it hid behind the guise of product development or "Product Promotions Engineering" and threw support where it best suited its needs. The flow of factory support for Bill began late in the summer of 1966, when Vince Piggins came knocking on the door. Bill remembers, "Initially it was nothing special, just some research and development work; nothing specific. Though the pay wasn't significant, cars and parts, over the years, were never an issue." Over time, most of Bill's dealings were with Paul Prior, an engineer who answered directly to Vince Piggins. Paul provided great help to Bill when it came to sourcing parts through different departments.

The New York International Raceway was the home of the Second Annual Super Stock Nationals held in July. Bill captured A/S class honors and brought home the Top Stock Eliminator crown. He defeated Tom Kerr in the finals with an easy 12.76-second pass. This proved to be the only major win for the Chevy II.

Top Stock at the Nationals was contested by 25 cars and in a scene repeated numerous times throughout the year; the final round came down to the street Hemi of Jere Stahl and the Chevy II of Jenkins. The previous day rumors had been circulating that Jenkins' Chevy II wasn't quite legal. Not helping matters, the night before the final, Jenkins and his crew paid a visit to three-time Indy 500 winner Mauri Rose, and used his garage to swap short blocks. Jenkins employee Charlie Strunk recalls, "The engine story actually began a couple weeks before the nationals when Grump said we should build another engine to take to Indy. We were using 6-inch Ansen rods in the good engine and Stahl knew about them. We were afraid he'd protest us if we beat him. It was too late to get ForgedTrue pistons so out came the 'junk.' We wound up putting a back-up cam in the engine, which had a different centerline. Turned out the cam really worked with the shorter, 5.7 rods."

Bruce Tucker reflected on the amount of thrashing taking place that weekend by saying, "We were rebuilding transmissions in hotel bathtubs, and

Bruce Tucker recalls many dreadful hours peeling factory sealant from every nook and cranny of this car over the winter of 1965–1966. The red stripes on the roof were a jab at the Ramchargers, which Bill took extra pleasure in beating. Over night, Jenkins division-one disciples followed suit. (Photo Courtesy Pete Gemar)

rebuilding rear carriers in waste baskets. It was a mess. Everything was done at the hotel because it was the only place you could work on the car."

It proved for naught. Bill caught the red light in the final round and handed Stahl the win.

When it came to building winning lower-class Stock champions, Jenkins Competition had no peers. Nine different cars guaranteed Jenkins' name made the winner's circle at Indy.

On the return trip from the Nationals, the Chevy II was destroyed in a towing accident on the Pennsylvania Turnpike. Crew member Bruce Tucker, driving the tow rig, passed out behind the wheel. Thankfully, there were no injuries in the incident, but the car was a complete write-off. The drivetrain was salvaged; what remained of the Chevy II was sent to a wrecking yard, where it sat for the next 20-plus years before being recycled.

Grumpy's Toy II, 1966 Chevy II

Bill purchased this second Chevy II from Penske Chevrolet and carried on from where the wrecked car had left off. This factory-white car was the start of a new trend for Bill; the white bodies stayed with him throughout his career. Why white all those years? Bill simply says, "Because they were cooler."

Fewer than 5,500 L79-equipped Chevy IIs were built in 1966, so even Bill Jenkins was hard-pressed to find a second one. The Nova (purchased with a 283-ci V-8) had the drivetrain from the wrecked car installed. Both of Jenkins' Chevy IIs were non-SS-model hardtops.

Drag News reported that the car had been completed prior to a match race against Jere Stahl on October 2 at Aquasco Raceway. Dressed in plain white paint, the Chevy II made its first pass, running an 11.56 at 119.00 mph. Jere went on to take the easy win after the Chevy II broke in the first round and could not be repaired in time to continue. Payback came two weeks later at Cecil County, when Bill won a best-of-five match race. The Chevy II turned an 11.11-second elapsed time at 123.19 mph on the final run, in contrast to Stahl's losing time of 11.26 at 125 mph even. *Drag News* said that the bus full of 42 adoring Grumpy fans that had made the trek from West Philadelphia went nuts, parading Bill on their shoulders.

Jere recalled the race, saying, "Bill and I had a gentlemen's agreement that we would match race legal. When Bill ripped off those low-11-second times, I knew he wasn't legal and eventually he admitted it to me. I had a new engine in the car that day. It was the first drag race engine to be honed while making use of a honing plate, and it also had a new "creative" legal compression ratio. It was the first Hemi built to the new NHRA specifications that I wrote for Chrysler following the Indy teardown debacle over the released dome volume specification. The new engine was capable of

The second Chevy II made its debut at Cecil County late in September, prior to the later match against Jere Stahl. Most parts salvaged from the wrecked car were used on this one. The Jenkins Competition advertisement hanging on the front bumper didn't last long; the NHRA asked Bill to remove it. (Bruce Tucker Collection)

running almost two tenths and 3 mph faster than the previous engine."

Jere went on to say, "Jenkins could really pull me in first gear. When I made the 1–2 shift with my 2.38 first gear, Bill was still in first with his 2.20 gear." Jere solved that problem by installing a set of 2:14 gears that he had previously purchased from Dave Strickler. These were Chrysler NASCAR road race gears that were used for the new process gear box. "We built the transmission to take to Tulsa for the World Finals. At the Finals, the track maintenance crew had scraped the racetrack clean, and traction was next to nil. I absolutely could not get a hold of the track in first gear with the 2.38 transmission, but when I installed the 2.14 transmission, the car left the line just right. It would barely bog, grab the track, and off I went." The NHRA Tulsa World Finals closed out the season and Jere's overpowering Hemi defeated

In the winter of 1966–1967, the little Chevy II could be seen running B/FX where Bill had the car nipping at the 10-second bracket. (Photo Courtesy David Smith)

Bill ran the Chevy II into April 1967 while preparing his new Camaro. Due to the initial lack of qualifying cars in the all-new Super Stock category, the Chevy II ran in Factory Experimental during a Cecil County outing. (Photo Courtesy David Smith)

Chapter Four

Bill en route to capturing the well-deserved World Championship.

Late in 1966, the NHRA announced that starting the following season, Super Stock was a separate category, and would no longer be lumped together with the Stock-class cars. The new rules allowed more freedom, including the use of any camshaft of choice and up to 10-inch-wide rear slicks. Anybody who has tried to squeeze 10-inch tires into a stock Chevy II wheel well knows it's impossible. Bill found that Oldsmobile Vista Cruiser station wagons used an offset that allowed him to squeeze a maximum 9 inches of tire under the car, and even that took some coaxing.

At the AHRA winter meet in January, Bill won the Middle Stock Eliminator crown with an 11.70 at 120.20 mph. The NHRA winter meet at Pomona wasn't so kind; Bill, running SS/C, fell early in eliminations.

The Chevy II was campaigned through the end of April 1967. Following a match race at Vargo Dragway, it was sold. In previous interviews, Bill had stated that, out of the box, this car ran equal to the red car it replaced and that he made some good money from the sale of this one. It seemed like King Midas; everything he touched turned to gold.

The Chevy II was sold to Joe Sediko of Jonestown, Pennsylvania, in the spring of 1967 and survives today. The semi-disassembled car is owned by a couple whose relationship ended years ago in a bitter divorce. They continue to butt heads while the Chevy II wastes away.

In late 1966 there was a reunion of sorts when Bill assembled a bored-and-stroked 427 for Dave Strickler's stretched-nose Experimental Stock "Funny" Corvette. Displacing 525 inches (4.3125-inch bore x 4½-inch stroke) *Old Reliable V* turned 8-second ETs running on 70-percent nitromethane.

Grumpy's Toy III, 1967 Camaro

Chevrolet introduced the Camaro in September 1966. It hoped to put a major dent in the pony car market, which Ford had created with its highly successful Mustang in the fall of 1964.

Jenkins' first Camaro came out of Chevrolet's research and development facility in Warren, Michigan, in December 1966. The Bolero Red SS 350 car was powered by the underrated 425-hp, 427-ci L-88 big-block. Though official talk of high performance was avoided at General Motors, Bill said, "It was the easiest way of getting me an L-88 at that point without direct shipping me one." Bill drove the car briefly, but quickly tired of continuously "fiddling" with the vacuum-assisted 850-cfm Holley carburetor. Frustrated with trying to get the secondaries to operate correctly, he pulled the linkage and ran them mechanically at a 1:1 ratio. Additional modifications included installing a secondary pump nozzle and

Hoping the new Camaro would catch on with the youth, Bill figured it would be the ideal drawing card. "But," he said, "Chevrolet really had nothing better to offer." (Photo Courtesy J. S. Elliot/Bruce Tucker Collection)

drilling passages so that the secondary "squirt" was coming in from the primary pump circuit (a trick he had learned back in the early 1960s, tuning Carter-carbureted 361-ci Chryslers). Holley later released its own version of the "center squirter" carburetor in 660- and 850-cfm sizes.

Eventually, an L-34 350-hp 396 was swapped into the Camaro prior to the car being sold. The L-88 powerplant was retained and used as the basis for a match race engine.

Late in March, Bill's right-hand man and engine builder, Joe Tryson, made the trek to the Chevrolet assembly plant in Norwood, Ohio, and took delivery of one of the first L78 396, 375-hp Camaros produced. As a heater- and radio-deleted car and with a 4.88:1 rear gear, it was a long, cold trip back to Pennsylvania for Joe.

Though limited by its own bureaucracy, Chevrolet protected its interests in drag racing. Because of Bill's close relationship with Vince Piggins and Paul Prior of Chevrolet's Racing Group, the 375-hp Camaro was built specifically to do battle in the new NHRA Super Stock category. There were ten classes in Super Stock, ranging from SS/A through to SS/E. There were five classes for manual transmission cars and five classes for automatic transmission cars. The class breakdowns were determined by vehicle weight divided by the NHRA-determined and factored horsepower rating. For a number of years, The Big Three had been falsifying horsepower ratings in hopes of gaining an advantage on the drag strip. By 1967, the NHRA had caught on to the scam and refactored the Camaro's advertised 375 hp to 425hp. Though it may have been a little slow at times, the NHRA was by no means ignorant and knew very well that this same engine had been used through 1965 and 1966 by Chevrolet and rated at 425 hp.

Super Stock eliminations came down to class winners, with the slower car getting the handicap start. If either driver ran quicker than .100 second below his class record, then he or she was automatically eliminated. It was common to see a cloud of tire smoke at the top end of the strip as drivers hit the brakes to slow the cars and ensure they didn't run too fast, or "break out" as it came to be known. Handicapping (or "brake light racing") was unanimously panned by Super Stock drivers, who almost immediately lobbied for a heads-up, no-break-out category.

In preparing the Camaro for Super Stock battle, the 396 went through the usual balancing and blueprinting. Jenkins' previously mentioned modifications were made to the 785-cfm Holley carb, which

Bill battles it out in Maryland with Hubert Platt in his Paul Harvey 427-powered Ford Fairlane. Bill dominated SS/C in the NHRA's Division One. (Photo Courtesy J. S. Elliot)

Chapter Four

fed the fuel through an extensively modified, Chevrolet factory intake manifold. They tried different camshafts in the big-block; Bill usually settled on either a General Kinetics or a Sig Erson bumpstick. They used factory forged pistons, squeezing out 12.5:1 compression.

Transmission choice came down to a Muncie case with either a 2.20, 2.36, or 2.54 first gear, depending on track conditions. Charlie Strunk recalls, "Grump could swap transmissions in 7 minutes or so. That's where the Super Crew phrase was coined. Prior to Borg-Warner producing the 2.36 first gear, Jenkins and company created their own using a combination of Ford and Chevy parts. The cluster gear had to be cut in half and lengthened, the main drive gear that goes into the clutch was cut, and a Chevy front was put on it. There were a couple of gears that had to have the center hole ground out to a larger size. Everything that was cut and welded had to be heat treated for hardness. I was running all over Philadelphia to find machine shops that could do the various operations. It really was a major project, and it was worth it." Gear changes were initially made using the same homemade shifter that Bill had used in the Chevy IIs. Oregon-based P&G was picked up as a sponsor during the season and Bill made use of the company's vertical gate, reverse lock-out shifter. The Camaro's 12-bolt rear generally carried either 4.56 or 4.88 gears.

Though it was illegal throughout all sanctioned drag race bodies, acid dipping parts was a common way of dropping unwanted vehicle weight. The subframe, radiator support, inner fenders, fenders, and trunk lid of *Grumpy's Toy III* spent time in the acid bath. Another weight-saving trick Bill used was to replace the steel front-end nuts and bolts (where possible) with lighter aluminum ones. These measures were repeated on *Grumpy's Toy IV* and *Grumpy's Toy VI*.

Cashing in on the popularity of the new Super Stock category, and answering the groans of the top drivers wanting to race heads-up, East Coast promoter Don Fissel was the first to present a heads-up Super Stock circuit. The format was simple: Follow the NHRA rules and run 13 races between June and October. There were no class runoffs; each event ran under the eliminations system. There were handicap starts, but there were no break-out rules.

By late in April, the Camaro was ready for the match race circuit, making its debut at Aquasco Raceway in Maryland. Turning times in the 11.20-second range, the L-88 427-powered Camaro came out on the short end of a three-way battle between ex–Funny Car pilot Ronnie Sox and eventual winner Jere Stahl. (Bruce Tucker Collection)

In the debut race at York US-30, Al Olster, in his Jenkins Competition–prepared *One Step Beyond* Plymouth, squared off against Bill in the final go. Al was a little too eager and caught a red light coming off the line, handing the win and $250 prize money to Bill, who had run a best time of 11.29. In October, Bill took the series crown, having earned the most wins.

Grumpy's Toy III made its debut in SS/C at the NHRA Springnationals, held at Bristol, Tennessee. Bill won the class with a best time of 11.77, but lost in eliminations to Ronnie Sox in his Hemi-powered Plymouth GTX.

After losing to Jere Stahl's street Hemi at the NHRA Nationals in 1966, Bill was seeking revenge in 1967. It wasn't easy; the competition was fierce. The

Jenkins' Camaro eventually ran an SS/C-class legal 10.96-second elapsed time at 128.80 mph, and held the class record numerous times throughout the year. (Bruce Tucker Collection)

Jenkins updated the Camaro late in 1967, incorporating the less-cluttered, lighter Rally Sport fascia. (Photo Courtesy J. S. Elliot/Bruce Tucker Collection)

Chapter Four

Against a stellar field of Ford and Chrysler products (as well as other Chevys), Jenkins waded through Monday's field to emerge victorious, taking Indy's first-ever Super Stock Eliminator title. A full story on the car ran in the January 1968 issue of Super Stock *magazine.* (Ray Mann Collection/www.quartermilestones.com)

Ed Hedrick earned his pay by playing runner-up in the Street Eliminator class with Grumpy's Toy III *at the NHRA World Finals.* (Bruce Tucker Collection)

Super Stockers: 1966–1969

Super Stock entry list read like a who's who of Super Stock royalty, with the best from across the country and Canada arriving in hopes of capturing the crown.

Chrysler and Ford had their A teams out in force. Sox & Martin, always a competitive threat, arrived with three Super Stock Mopars prepared to do battle. In a move that raised many eyebrows, Dave Strickler temporarily parked his "funny" Corvette and wheeled a Hemi GTX for the Sox & Martin camp. Bob Brown (in his SS/A record-holding 1965 Plymouth) was there along with Arlen Vanke, who reportedly showed up with five cars. Ron Mancini, Mary Ann Foss, and Don Grotheer were all present with their Chryslers. Of course Jere Stahl made the show in a Belvedere II, hoping for a repeat of the previous year.

Ford pinned its hopes on the 427-powered Fairlane platform and its drivers Ed Terry, Don Nicholson, Hubert Platt, and Jerry Harvey.

Bill Jenkins and Dick Arons each brought in Camaros and Wally Booth entered his 1966 Chevelle. These were only a few of the notable Chevrolet stalwarts.

As reported in *Super Stock & Drag Illustrated*, as eliminations progressed, the Chryslers and Fords defeated each other. By the third round, the Fords had all been eliminated. Hubert Platt's 10.96-second low elapsed time of the meet did him no good in the land of handicap racing.

Bill Jenkins, operating with the precision of a Swiss watch, had driven his way to the final round with times as quick as 11.45. There, he met Bob Brown and his much quicker Plymouth. With a handicap start, Bill took the lead on Bob and never looked back. He took the win with an 11.55-second pass at 115.97 mph to a quicker-but-losing 11.10-second run at 125.52 mph. Bill downplayed his first national event win behind the wheel of a Chevrolet, but at the same time he made clear what he thought of the existing Super Stock format by saying the win was luck. "In handicap racing, that's what it comes down to."

At the 1968 NHRA Winternationals, Bill defeated Hubert Platt's 427-powered Fairlane for SS/C class honors with an 11.18 at 125.87 mph. He then lost to the 480-ci 1967 Camaro driven by *Hot Rod* magazine managing editor Don Evans. The magazine had

At the 1968 NHRA Winternationals, Super Stock odds were stacked against Bill (and pretty much every other competitor) as Ford dominated with its newly released 428-powered Mustang. Bill won his class with Grumpy's Toy III, *while Al Joneic took home all the marbles. Note the hand-painted Hooker Headers logo. Bill was credited with designing the iconic logo, which is still in use today.* (Photo Courtesy Jim Handy)

Chapter Four

Grumpy's Camaro briefly held the A/MP class record with a 10.68-second pass at 131.19 mph. (Bruce Tucker Collection)

Bill tuning the 850-cfm Holley carbs at the 1968 NHRA World Finals, while a young Joe Tryson and Ed Hedrick look on. (Photo Courtesy John Eichinger)

taken possession of the pre-production car from Chevrolet's engineering group in Arizona, and decided to prepare the car for some class action. Bill Thomas was commissioned to build what *Hot Rod* editor Jim McFarland had believed to be an NHRA-legal 325-horse 396-ci engine. He didn't know what he was really getting.

Staging together for the class runoff, Jenkins left Evans on the line with two yellow bulbs remaining on the tree. The *Hot Rod* Camaro waited for the solid green bulb and made a half-pass down the track. Jim McFarland, who had entered the event just to gain some exposure for Chevrolet, immediately headed for the timing tower and withdrew the Camaro, practically begging Jack Hart to reinstate Jenkins. It was fruitless to argue with Jack and the losing red light stood, to the delight of the Ford and Chrysler representatives waiting for word at the base of the tower.

It wasn't until the Bakersfield meet in March that the *Hot Rod* crew discovered the engine actually displaced 480 (illegal) inches.

In July 1968, Bill made a forgettable appearance at the Super Stock Nationals, running heads-up with the car, and being quickly eliminated. Jenkins' crew member Pete Preston, a very capable driver in his own right, drove the SS/C *Grumpy's Toy IV* Camaro at the same event, but retired early after losing a transmission.

At the NHRA Nationals in September, *Grumpy's Toy III* ran SS/C and won its class, but lost in the third round of eliminations after being chased down by "Akron" Arlen Vanke.

The same month, *Car Craft* magazine held its first annual awards banquet, called the All Star Drag Racing Team Awards. This event generally took place the same weekend as the Nationals, and honored those chosen by the reading public and a select panel as "the best" in a specific drag-racing-related category. In a preview of things to come, Bill made his first trip to the podium, accepting awards for Super Stock driver and Stock engine builder.

Grumpy's Toy III made its final appearance at the NHRA World Finals in 1968. Running in the A/Modified Production class, Ed Hedrick drove the car to the runner-up position in Street Eliminator, losing out to Fred Hurst's Barracuda with a 10.60-second time at 132.74 mph. The 427-ci engine that had been installed for the meet sported a pair of pre-production, cast-iron, open-chamber heads topped by the new Edelbrock tunnel ram manifold. A pair of "too large" 850-cfm Holley carburetors topped the engine.

Gary Kimball purchased *Grumpy's Toy III*, along with a Jenkins-prepared L-88 engine, and campaigned

The restored Grumpy's Toy III *at the York Reunion in 2003.* (Author Collection)

Chapter Four

the car on the AHRA heads-up Super Stock circuit. Kimball wreaked havoc there, winning nearly every event entered and earning the points title along with $30,000 in the process.

As of this writing, *Grumpy's Toy III* is in the hands of a private collector and has been restored to its former SS/C status.

George Cureton's *Tokyo Rose*

The Jenkins mystique started in the 1950s and as his reputation for building winning Stock-class racers spread, Bill became the go-to guy in the tri-state area. He says, "Things got serious around 1963 and, really, it was just an evolution of what I had started back in 1955 when I set out on my own." In 1963, Jenkins was doing major tune-ups on 409-powered cars at $500 to $600 a pop. For the money, the customer could count on the cam timing being adjusted, the distributor being re-curved, the cylinder heads reworked and cc'd, and a reworking of the carburetors. With Bill running his own car in 1966, time became a factor and he had to be more selective about what work he took on.

In 1967, Delaware resident George Cureton captured the NHRA World Championship. He drove his Jenkins-prepared G/SA 1956 Chevrolet sedan delivery.

George Cureton's NHRA World Champion *Tokyo Rose* comes off the line at Cecil County, circa 1968. Building a truly competitive car for the lower Stock classes was not cheap. (Photo Courtesy Michael "Mashie" Mihalko)

Super Stockers: 1966–1969

George's first serious venture into drag racing came in 1965 behind the wheel of an I/SA 1955 Chevy. Though it didn't run too bad, he distinctively recalls continuously being frustrated by Ed Beyer's Pontiac. George sold the 1955 the following year and purchased the 265-powered sedan delivery, which he prepared for NHRA Stock-class competition.

Fellow Delaware racer Alex Jarrell was a guiding force in George's drag racing career. Alex happened to be a friend and customer of Bill Jenkins and, through this connection, George had Jenkins build an engine for the sedan delivery. George provided the block and heads, and Bill supplied the rest. A complete Jenkins Competition small-block for a Chevy Stocker, from carburetor to oil pan, was worth $2,500 to $3,000. This was not cheap by any means, but for the money you received an engine that was guaranteed to run under the class record the first time out.

Outside of winning the World Championship, one of the most memorable moments for George was beating the record. Though the exact elapsed time isn't on record, George distinctly remembers the car ran well under the G/SA record.

George recalls how he and Bill always seemed to be at the same track at the same time, and that "he always paid attention to the car, standing behind the line watching the car run. If he felt the car wasn't running right, or if he picked up on something while watching you, he'd tell you. He wouldn't necessarily fix it for you, but he'd tell you what needed to be done. You'd do it, and it would work." George recalls that the sedan delivery was apart many times being protested, "At $50 a pop, I made a lot of money, as it always proved to be legal."

Though he planned to call the car *Big Orange*, the paint applied to cover the sedan delivery's original black didn't turn out quite the way George had hoped. "We mixed a Mustang orange with a metallic, which I thought would come out a metallic orange, but it came out a rose color. I kind of liked the oriental theme, so that's how the *Tokyo Rose* name came about."

The car was damaged one evening while being flat towed to Capitol Raceway in Maryland. The choice was to either be forced off of the road by an errant driver, or drive into the median. George chose the median and caused extensive damage to the car when it rolled onto its side. The car was repaired, and then painted the more familiar marina-blue color.

George sold the car in 1969, and replaced it with a fuel-injected M/SA1958 Pontiac, figuring "that was the way to go." Apparently it wasn't; the car showed little success and was sold after only one season. He found greater success after he purchased Bobby Warren's NHRA World Finals-winning Chevy Nova. George's final race car, before retiring from drag racing in 1980, was a 1966 L/SA class Chevy II.

George Cureton still lives in Delaware at the time of this writing. He is enjoying his retirement and the horse racing track. Outside of the Spanakos' *Monster Mash* Chevys, Bill stated (for obvious reasons) that *Tokyo Rose* was one of the cars he was most proud of.

Grumpy's Toy IV, 1968 Camaro

Bill decided to run multiple cars in 1968, so he purchased a second Camaro through Ammon R. Smith. The car arrived sporting an aluminum-head L-89 engine and butternut-yellow paint. Bill had considered changing from his patented white because photographers continuously complained of the white cars "burning up" the photos. Bill had a change of mind, and body-man Dan Carlucci repainted the car his trademark white.

Grumpy's Toy IV made its debut in April at Englishtown, New Jersey, during a heads-up Super Stock event. Driver Ed Hedrick was defeated in the first round by Bill Blanding's SS/EA Camaro.

Ed Hedrick, who was coming off a Championship year driving his B/-, C/-, and D/SP-winning Shelby Cobra, was looking for a ride in 1968; new rules more or less made his Cobra uncompetitive. Though Bill and Ed were acquainted at the track, they also shared a mutual friendship with Jere Stahl, who suggested to Ed that he talk to Bill about driving the second car. This collaboration led to both Bill and Ed buying into Stahl's performance store, upon Dick Moroso's departure in 1968. Each retained 15-percent ownership until the doors closed in 1974. Though Bill had little hands-on involvement in the store, he did have Borg-Warner produce high-nickel gears (producing various ratios) that sold through what came to be known as Stahl & Associates.

Ed made his debut late in February, driving *Grumpy's Toy III* during a divisional meet at Aquasco Raceway in Maryland. Ed wasn't used to the slick shift transmission. He recalls letting off the gas pedal during gear changes, "I bent the accelerator

Chapter Four

On a dollar-made-versus-dollar-invested basis, this was, by far, the most profitable of the Grumpy's Toys. It returned approximately $150,000, over three years, on his $8,000 investment. (Photo Courtesy J. S. Elliot/Bruce Tucker Collection)

pump lever on the Holley from whacking on and off the gas pedal." After settling in, Ed went on to win the Super Stock Eliminator with 11.0-second elapsed times.

Super Stock magazine ran its Fourth Annual Nationals at Cecil County and followed AHRA's lead by running a heads-up Super Stock category. Referred to as "Experimental Super Stock" (X/SS), the rules were similar to those run at the previous AHRA Winter meet. Cars were limited to American-made sedans no more than 2 years old, with the engine maximum of 430 ci. All Chrysler Hemi-equipped cars had to run at 3,400 pounds, while all tunnel-port-equipped Fords had to weigh 3,300 pounds. The big-block Chevy-powered cars had to weigh 3,200 pounds. If you were attempting to run anything smaller, well, you probably didn't stand a chance. Cars were limited to the stock wheelbase, the stock wheel wells, and a maximum of two carburetors. Everything else was a go.

Ed Hedrick drove for Bill, running the 1967 car powered by an iron-block 427-ci engine, but fouled away his chances in the quarter finals with a starting line red light, leaving the door open for rival Sox & Martin. In what can only be described as a bizarre twist of the rules, Ronnie Sox had also pulled a red light on the run, but, because he had the lower elapsed time, he was allowed to advance. Sox & Martin won the event with a 10.34-second elapsed time. Not to come home empty handed, the Jenkins-prepared SS/F Camaro of Dave Strickler captured class honors.

By the summer of 1968, Bill had outgrown the two rear bays of Ollie's Sonoco and made a move to nearby Malvern. He leased a building for the next five years before having his own built. Due to an increase in mail theft, Jenkins found it necessary to have all deliveries sent to a neighboring address, just to ensure he received them.

Bill prepared three cars to do battle at the NHRA Nationals in September. *Grumpy's Toy III* was qualified by Ed Hedrick in SS/C with a 10.98-second ET, which was immediately protested by the Chrysler fraternity. But the L-78–powered car proved legal and, with Jenkins driving, won its class. But Bill lost in eliminations to the all-too-familiar Arlen Vanke. The 1968 Camaro, *Grumpy's Toy IV*, was driven by Dave Strickler in the A/MP class, powered by an L-88. Ed Hedrick drove the L-78–powered 1968 Nova in the SS/D classification. Other than having three cars at the race, it was a forgettable weekend; Ed and Dave were eliminated early in competition.

At the *Car Craft* magazine awards banquet, Bill accepted the award for Super Stock driver and Stock engine builder. Though impossible to verify now, it has previously been reported that, between 1965 and 1968, cars prepared by Jenkins Competition were responsible for an average of 20 class records per year, with the majority being lower Stock-class Chevys.

In October, Jenkins Competition made a grand entrance at the NHRA World Finals at Tulsa, Oklahoma, arriving with four cars in tow; three of Bill's own (including the SS/D Nova) and the Super Stock/F Z/28 Camaro of Dave Strickler. In a reversal of the Nationals, *Grumpy's Toy III* ran A/MP while *Grumpy's Toy IV* ran SS/C with the L-78 engine.

Bill drove the Nova throughout the event while Ed Hedrick hopped back and forth between the two Camaros. In the Super Stock final, Dave Strickler's Z/28 defeated the Nova with a 11.80 at 116.20 mph to a losing 11.48 at 120.64 mph. Either way, it was a win-win situation for Jenkins Competition.

Grumpy's Toy IV was match raced late in 1968 and into the 1969 season, making use of the Chaparral 427 aluminum block. Bill had received two of these blocks from Chevrolet late in 1968. Chevrolet had developed the aluminum 427 block late in 1966, in conjunction with Jim Hall for use in his Chaparral race cars. These aluminum cylinder blocks were available to select racers through Chevrolet's Performance Group, and it's believed that Bill was the only one in drag racing to make use of the engine. Excluding the weight savings, Jenkins felt there was no advantage in using the Chaparral over the iron block.

By the end of the 1968 season, many drivers, including Bill, "Dyno Don" Nicholson, and the team of Sox & Martin, were fed up with the current Super Stock "run too fast and you lose" format. They approached the NHRA seeking a professional heads-up category. Buddy Martin was the spokesperson on behalf of the group and proposed rules that would be similar to those run at the recent Super Stock Nationals. The engine would have to be of the same manufacture as the body and would be limited to a

What once held so much promise—the Stahl-Moroso store in York, Pennsylvania, circa 1968. The relationship deteriorated, and Dick Moroso moved on. His shares were bought by Jim Hopkinson and Bill Jenkins, who would partner with existing shareholders Jim Kerr, Ed Hedrick, and, of course, Jere Stahl. (Photo Courtesy Phil Cooper)

Dave Strickler borrowed a rig from Ammon R. Smith and made the 1968 Super Stock Nationals in style. It's a shame the race didn't turn out as nice for either him or Jenkins. (Photo Courtesy Jerry MacNeish)

Chapter Four

maximum of 427 ci. No superchargers or fuel injectors were permitted, though any carburetor, intake manifold, and camshaft would be acceptable. Hood scoops and lightweight body panels would also be permitted and all cars, regardless of engine, and they would carry the same minimum weight of 2,800 pounds. The NHRA balked at the idea and drivers had to wait another year before the leading sanctioning body implemented a heads-up category of its own.

In mid 1969, Bill headed up to Detroit Dragway, where Chevrolet plugged *Grumpy's Toy IV* into its mobile instrumentation van. Bill recalls the interior of the Camaro being packed with instrumentation, data-recording equipment, and telemetry stuff that was required to broadcast the data so it could be picked up by the van. In his book *Chevrolet Racing: Fourteen Years of Raucous Silence!*, Paul Van Valkenburgh stated, "A typical recording might include engine speed, individual rear-wheel speeds, engine torque, and axle torque." Though it's a given that horsepower is lost through the drivetrain, Paul said that it was an unexpected amount of horsepower being lost. This led to further investigation into drivetrain efficiency. The data also found that the engine over-revved quite a bit more than expected in wide-open-throttle speed shifting. Regardless of the quickness of the driver, declutching at a 7,200-rpm shift point allows the engine to spike up to almost 9,000 rpm.

Overall, each felt there wasn't a lot learned from the tests, though Bill elaborated, saying at the time there was no relative data to go on. Experience gained in regard to what you could and could not get away with, and how things had to be done, have to be relevant to what you had to do in a road race or circle track car. It was an experience for everyone but there wasn't any immediate performance gained, because too little data existed for comparison.

At the Fifth Annual Super Stock Nationals held at York, Bill won the Experimental Super Stock class with *Grumpy's Toy IV*. He recorded the fastest time of the event while downing the Barracuda of Sox & Martin. Jenkins posted a 9.94-second pass at 141.93 mph to Sox's 10.13 at 135 mph. This was the first sub-10-second time ever recorded by a Super Stock car.

At the NHRA Nationals in September 1969, Bill ran *Grumpy's Toy IV* in B/Gas. He had done this on and off through the season for no other reason than it was another class to run. An aluminum-block Chaparral 427, sporting a Weiand tunnel ram and a

The Wheatley brothers supplied the truck to haul Grumps Group to the Nationals in 1968. Top left, Brad Watkins; right, Alex Jarrell; bottom row, Jay and Buck Wheatley. (Photo Courtesy Michael "Mashie" Mihalko)

Super Stockers: 1966–1969

The 1968 Camaro ran numerous categories through 1970, including the previously mentioned Super Stock, Gas, match race, and finally Pro Stock. (Photo Courtesy Sal Marino)

At the 1968 NHRA World Finals in Tulsa, Oklahoma, Bill drove Grumpy's Toy IV *to class honors. Here, Bill prepares the Camaro with assistance from Joe Tryson.* (Photo Courtesy John Eichinger)

Chapter Four

At the 1969 NHRA Winternationals, the Camaro ran SS/D and won its class, but bowed out in the first round of eliminations to Jerry Harvey's SS/I 428-powered Mustang. (Photo Courtesy Bob McClurg)

Jay Wheatley, in his N/SA 1955 Chevrolet sedan delivery, makes another mid-14-second pass during a Division One points meet at Maple Grove. Brothers Jay and Buck Wheatley had long-term success running engines prepared by Jenkins Competition. (Photo Courtesy Car Rubrecht)

Super Stockers: 1966–1969

Once again, Grumpy's Toy IV *grabs class honors. This was at the 1969 NHRA Winternationals.* (Photo Courtesy Bob McClurg)

pair of 850-cfm Holleys, propelled the car to low-10-second times. Dave Strickler did him one better by making a 10.00-flat pass while running the Camaro at Maple Grove.

By year's end, Jenkins shocked the likes of Don Nicholson and Ronnie Sox, turning match race times in the 9.70-second range with the Camaro using the Chaparral 427.

The Camaro's final incarnation was as a Pro Stocker, making its debut at the NHRA Winternationals in 1970.

The Camaro was powered by a 430-ci aluminum Can-Am engine, a few of which Bill had received in mid 1969. As qualifying got underway during this inaugural event, Ronnie Sox (in the all-new Sox & Martin Hemi Barracuda) nailed down the number-1 qualifying position with a 10-second-flat elapsed time. Bill, in *Grumpy's Toy IV*, grabbed the second spot with a 10.08 at 139.31mph. Less than half a second covered the field, as the sixteenth and final qualifier (Sam Auxier, Jr., in his Boss-powered Maverick) ran an elapsed time of 10.49-seconds.

On his march to a final-round appearance, Bill eliminated Bill "Mr. Bardahl" Hielscher, Mike Fons, and a red-lighting "Dandy" Dick Landy in his 16-plug Hemi-powered Dodge Challenger. In four of the five elimination runs, the Camaro produced 9-second times.

The reported crowd of 90,000 watched Bill pin a 9.99 final-round defeat of Ronnie Sox, who came up short with a 10.12-second run. Bill's 139.55-mph posting on the final run proved to be the top speed of the meet.

This was proving to be a costly trip for Californians. A week later at Orange County, for the United States Pro Stock Championship, Bill steered the Camaro through a 16-car field. He defeated Don Nicholson and his 427-powered Maverick in the

Grumpy's Toy IV *ran B/Gas at the NHRA Nationals in 1969. This same year, word came down from Chevrolet to lose the Jenkins Competition Bowtie logo design. Officially, Chevrolet was not involved in racing!* (Photo Courtesy Bob Plumer)

Grumpy's Toys 81

Chapter Four

Heads-up, four-across drag racing is making a comeback, but it's not a new idea. Here, at York Dragway in July 1969. Bill turned a 9.84-second pass while shutting down "Dyno" Don Nicholson, Steve Kanuika, and Ronnie Sox. (Photo Courtesy Jeff Tinsley)

As these vintage photos show, between 1963 and 1968, Jenkins Competition was located in Berwyn, Pennsylvania, making use of the rear bays of this Sonoco station. (Photo Courtesy Phil Cooper)

final go, with a 9.87 to a red-light 9.93. Bill went home with a best of 139.96 mph and both ends of the Orange County International Raceway track record. Total two-week earnings for the not-so-Grumpy one approached $20,000.

The next stop was Florida, where the First Annual NHRA Gatornationals were held in mid February. Once again Grumpy's Camaro held down the number-2 qualifying position, behind the 'Cuda of Sox & Martin, with a 9.81 to Sox's 9.79. And once

Bill is not the type who disposes of things quickly. The 1965 El Camino served him for more than 30 years, and the old Chevy panel was his work truck dating back to the turn of the decade. Note the match-race-prepped *Grumpy's Toy III* to the left. (Photo Courtesy Phil Cooper)

In what many considered an upset, Jenkins put away the favored Hemi 'Cuda of Sox & Martin in the final go. (Photo Courtesy www.LesWelch.com)

Chapter Four

Dick Landy and his new-for-1970 Challenger fouled to Jenkins in the second round of eliminations. Bill would go on to turn his second 9.98 time of the meet. (Photo Courtesy www.LesWelch.com)

Looking a little aloof, Jenkins grabs the Wally (and the girl), capturing the inaugural Pro Stock win. (Photo Courtesy www.LesWelch.com)

Super Stockers: 1966–1969

again, the pair met in the final round. To reach the finals, Jenkins had to wade through Hubert Platt, Bill Stepp, and Dick Landy. On the other side of the fence, Sox defeated Dick Loehr, Herb McCandless, and Don Carlton. Leaving Sox on the line, Jenkins captured his second national-event win, beating Ronnie on a holeshot with a 9.90-second time to a quicker-but-losing 9.86-second pass.

Bill capped off the month with a trip to Detroit Raceway, where he match raced Sam Auxier, Jr., and his Boss-powered Mustang. Jenkins defeated Sam in three straight runs, to close out the month with close to $30,000 in earnings.

Bill has stated that the 1968 car was always one of his favorites (for obvious reasons), and at one time he considered buying the car back after tracking it down in north Jersey in the early 2000s. The car needed a complete restoration; it had reportedly been heavily modified over the years.

A shot from the Division One awards banquet in 1968. Left to right are Super Stock recipient Dave Strickler, a woozy-looking Bill Jenkins, Jim McCraw (who was then editor of Super Stock & Drag Illustrated *magazine), and Stock Champ Bill Izykowski.* (Darwin Doll Collection)

Proudly representing Jenkins Competition at the NHRA Winternationals in Pomona, California, circa 1970. (Photo Courtesy Pat Smith/www.turboracingphotos.com)

At the NHRA Winternationals in 1969, it appears the Grump may have a smile on his face. (Photo Courtesy Bob McClurg)

A look at Ed Franks out of Trenton, New Jersey, and his record-holding L/Stock 1957 Chevrolet. The Franks/Green/Bixby team, in their Jenkins-prepared 270-hp 283-powered 1957, were frequent winners in the Northeast. (Photo Courtesy Carl Rubrecht)

Chapter Four

The aging Camaro beat all comers at the OCIR Pro Stock Championship in 1970. (Photo Courtesy Pat Smith/www.turboracingphotos.com)

Bill runs his Camaro through the rosin, aiming to repeat his Winternationals win at the first annual Pro Stock Championships held at Orange County International Raceway. (Photo Courtesy Bob McClurg)

Grumpy's Toy V, 1968 Chevy II

The 1968 Chevy II/Nova made its debut in March. It competed in the NHRA SS/D class with an L-78 396-ci, 375-hp engine. The L-79 327 car was pulled off of the assembly line and used by Chevrolet's engineering group as a test mule at its Warren, Michigan, facility.

Comparatively speaking, the Nova wasn't used much; Jenkins concentrated most of his efforts on the two Camaros. (Ed Hedrick Collection)

Jenkins entered 1968 with his sights on winning the Championship. So he hired Ed Hedrick to drive one of the three cars campaigned that year. (Jere Stahl Collection)

Super Stockers: 1966–1969

In 1968, Chevrolet advertised the L-78 396-powered Nova as the "Toughest Block on the Block." The Jenkins/Hedrick team went out and proved it by running record setting mid-11-second ETs. (Photo Courtesy Tom Schiltz)

Instead of scrapping the car when done testing, which was the usual final demise of such vehicles, the Nova was offered to Bill in hopes he could do something with it. Chevrolet wanted the Nova, with its new body style, to be seen in action by the young people they hoped would be buying it.

Bill made the trek to Warren to take delivery of the Nova and said that the car was never raced with the L-79 engine. What became of the original engine once it was swapped out for the 396 is long forgotten. The car was never match raced and, compared to the two Camaros that were also run in 1968, the Nova actually saw little use.

In June, Ed Hedrick piloted the Nova to SS/D class honors at the NHRA Springnationals.

Prior to the Tulsa meet in October, the car set the class record with an 11.45-second elapsed time. Ed Hedrick recalls the quickest time turned by the car was its 11.17-second qualifying time at the NHRA Indy Nationals.

At the World Finals in Tulsa, Bill and the Nova were defeated in the final round by Dave Strickler's Z/28. Ed Hedrick noted that history might have recorded different results if the Nova's rear end hadn't slipped off the leaf-spring centering pin, causing the wheel to make contact with the body on that final run.

Paul Seisler purchased Grumpy's Nova at the end of the 1968 season. He renamed it Sir Tiger *and ran in the NHRA SS/E class.* (Photo Courtesy Carl Rubrecht)

Ed Hedrick, having proven his prowess the previous season behind the wheel of his own car, was hired by Bill in 1968, and did the majority of his driving in the Nova. (Ed Hedrick Collection)

Grumpy's Toys 87

Chapter Four

Ed Hedrick warms the hides at Island Dragway in New Jersey. The Nova was sold at the end of the 1968 season, and has reportedly spent its life as a race car in the northeastern United States. (Photo Courtesy J. S. Elliot, Bruce Tucker Collection)

Dave Strickler's *Old Reliable*, 1968 Camaro

In 1968, Jenkins Competition prepared a Corvette Bronze Z/28 Camaro for Dave Strickler to run in the NHRA SS/F classification. A near-identical show car was also built and spent its time either parked in the showroom of Ammon R. Smith or making the rounds with the Strickler-Jenkins Car Clinic.

The highlight of the racing car's career (and possibly Dave's) came in October 1968 at the NHRA World Finals in Tulsa, Oklahoma. Dave captured Super Stock honors and the World Championship, defeating the Grump and his SS/D Nova with an 11.80-second elapsed time. Earlier the same month, Dave pushed the Camaro to a sub-record time of 11.73-seconds while winning a heads-up match at Englishtown, New Jersey.

The Camaro's drivetrain consisted of a 0.30-inch overbored Jenkins-built 302-ci small-block, producing approximately 450 hp. It was backed up by a Muncie M-22 transmission and 5.38:1 rear gears.

In 1969, the car received a very-low-buck coat of white paint courtesy of K-Mart-brand spray cans. The 302 was replaced with a Jenkins-prepped iron block 427-ci big-block and the car was match raced, producing low 10-second quarter-mile times.

Strickler sold the Camaro in 1970 to Harry Wyble, who ran the car in the Pro Stock category for one season with little success.

John Hasell purchased the car from Harry in the early 1980s and went bracket racing for a number of years before current owner Jerry McNeish came along in 1993 and bought the car, then restoring it

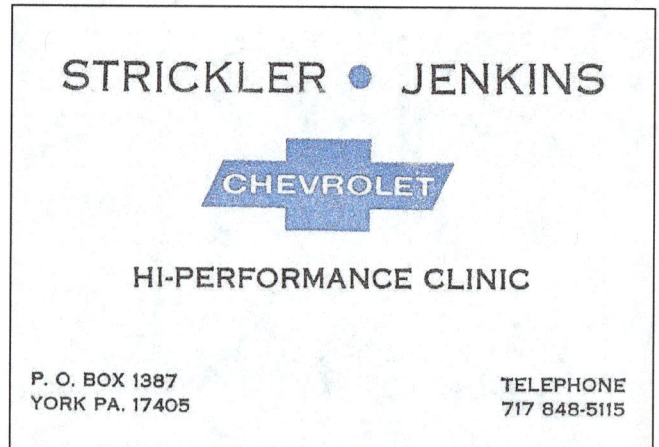

The Strickler-Jenkins High-Performance Clinic ran approximately two years and traveled as far away as Texas. The clinic, modeled after Chrysler's Clinic program, had cars built specifically for the traveling road show. (Bill Jenkins Collection)

back to its former *Old Reliable* status. Jerry campaigned the car as an NHRA Stocker and captured numerous class wins along with winning two divisional points meets. The car was finally retired from its life of racing in 2007.

The late Dave Strickler poses proudly with his NHRA World-Championship-winning SS/F Z/28 Camaro. The Corvette bronze paint was a rarity on the Camaro. (Photo Courtesy Mike Strickler)

Dave's Camaro, seen here in 1969 at Numidia Dragway. The car was match raced through the year before being sold off in 1970. (Photo Courtesy Carl Rubrecht)

Chapter Four

Jerry McNeish puts the Old Reliable *Camaro through its paces at Englishtown in 1995. The car has since been retired from duty.* (Photo Courtesy Jerry McNeish)

Grumpy's Toy VI, 1969 Camaro

Jenkins purchased the latest *Toy* through Roth Chevrolet in Paoli, Pennsylvania, and submitted the bill to Chevrolet for reimbursement. It was manufactured with an L-78 396-ci engine but, for the 2½-year campaign in which it served as *Grumpy's Toy*, the car was raced with a pair of 427-ci big-blocks.

The car made its debut in March, match racing and defeating the likes of Bill Stiles, Sam Auxier, Jr., and George Weller, while powered by a stock-bore Chaparral 427. By month's end, the Camaro was turning 10.20-second times at 133 mph. Jenkins commented, "We were match racing up to three times a week, pulling in $2,000 to $3,000 per race by this point. Generally, we were running two cars and the only time we paused was to run national events to keep the sponsors happy."

Contrary to popular belief, Bill never ran a ZL-1 in competition, preferring instead to use the Chaparral and later the Can-Am block. Bill had a low opinion of the ZL-1 block, referring to it as junk. He claims there was just too much movement in the ZL-1 blocks and they sealed poorly. As the aluminum blocks in general were susceptible to temperature fluctuations, Bill rigged up a pump so hot water could continuously be circulated through the engines between rounds to help maintain a constant 140 degrees F. Block heaters were installed as a way of maintaining temperature overnight. Due to the high wear rate, Jenkins replaced the piston rings after every dozen or so runs.

At the NHRA Springnationals (held in Dallas, Texas, during June), the Chaparral-powered Camaro failed technical inspection due to the unqualified aluminum block. The Chrysler guys, including engineers who happened to be at the race, had protested the ZL-1. They questioned whether the required number of factory cars equipped with the alloy block had been produced.

Jenkins said, "Back then, they [NHRA] weren't too picky about which block you ran, so we bolted an intake and carb on the Chaparral and called it a ZL-1." Jenkins was told by the NHRA that more proof was required—showing 50 Z-L1 cars were not only produced but had been sold.

Grumpy remembers, "Vince Piggins (or an employee of his product promotions group) had to go around to Chevrolet dealers and collect the information to prove to the NHRA that the cars were, in fact, sold." Jenkins had no choice but to park the Camaro and, as planned, run *Grumpy's Toy IV* in the Street Eliminator class.

Chevrolet's Tonawanda engine plant would provide Jenkins with a few Can-Am blocks. These were preferred over the ZL-1 and Chaparral units due to its larger 4.4375-inch bore, better sleeve fit, and better-quality alloy. Jenkins made use of the blocks in some late-season match races and they became the basis for his Pro Stock engines in 1970. Producing approximately 600 hp, the engines featured 12:5.1 compression, open-chamber heads, and a pair of Holley 650-cfm carbs, which were twisted 90 degrees

Super Stockers: 1966–1969

Grumpy's Toy VI *at the York Super Stock Nationals in 1970—always one of my favorites.* (Photo Courtesy Bob Plumer)

Larry Lombardo driving his Roger Sinistri–prepared F/Stock 1961 Corvette. Lombardo won the NHRA US Nationals in 1968. Larry's prowess behind the wheel caught Jenkins' attention. (Photo Courtesy Carl Rubrecht)

Jenkins versus Lombardo at Maple Grove, circa 1969. Within a few years, Lombardo took over behind the wheel of Grumpy's Toy. (Photo Courtesy Carl Rubrecht)

During a moment of rest at the 1969 NHRA Springnationals, Bill lent a hand to Ed Hedrick and his 427-powered Camaro. In an uncharacteristic move, Ed overstaged in the first round of class eliminations, fouled, and was disqualified. This brought a quick end to a promising weekend. (Photo Courtesy John Eichinger)

Another photo of Grumpy's Toy VI, shot during the summer of 1969 at a Maple Grove points meet. The Jenkins Competition decal design was changed in 1969, after Chevrolet insisted Jenkins lose the Bowtie. (Photo Courtesy Carl Rubrecht)

Chapter Four

and mounted on a Weiand tunnel-ram intake manifold. Mounting the carburetors sideways allowed for removal of the bowls without having to remove the carburetors from the manifold. Additionally, Jenkins found it seemed to help prevent fuel starvation during acceleration.

In a move first attempted on the Can-Am blocks to aid piston ring seal, Bill had pressure relief holes (or gas ports) drilled through the deck of the pistons to the top ring land, behind the ring. The idea was that the top ring would have the added benefit of compression pressure from behind. This was to aid in expansion and the seal against the cylinder wall.

As Bill explained, "We tried it first with the vertical clearance of the rings at the more conventional .002 inch, but nothing really happened until we tightened the clearance, and we didn't get around to that until 1971. Basically, the relief holes didn't work at first so we invented something so that they would." Vertical clearance was brought down to .0006–.001 and the volume-enhancing groove was added. As Bill noted in his book *The Chevrolet Racing*

With **Grumpy's Toy VI** failing to pass inspection at the NHRA Springnationals in Dallas, Bill ran the Street Eliminator class with **Grumpy's Toy IV**. He failed to make an impact, losing out during class eliminations. (Photo Courtesy John Eichinger)

Many different combinations were used during the first year of Pro Stock competition. Here, Bill is seen during first-round action at the 1970 NHRA Springnationals at Dallas International Motor Speedway. His opponent, Joe Ralph Thompson of Arkansas, is in one of Dodge's Hurst-built 1968 Hemi-powered Darts. (Jon Steele Archive/www.quartermilestones.com)

Engine, "If vertical clearance is reduced too much, the ring will not operate properly because it relies heavily upon the gas pressure developed during combustion for correct sealing. We had reached the condition where we had the ring stacks shoved together, vertically. There wasn't any volume left between the first and second ring, and it was getting into the condition where we were wearing out the top of the top ring more than the bottom because of a secondary reaction between the two rings. It was upsetting the ring, driving it into the top land on the piston and causing a wear issue, leading to excessive blow by. We put the groove in to get the volume between the rings back, and it worked."

The groove was cut into the space between the top and second ring. This innovation was one of the few things Bill wished he had patented; eventually it was incorporated by more than one auto manufacturer.

At the NHRA US Nationals, Bill ran the Camaro in SS/C and qualified in the number-2 position behind the 1965 Plymouth of "Akron" Arlen Vanke. Jenkins' 10.72-second elapsed time was run in vain when he caught a red light in the very first round of

Bill prepares for a match race against Sox & Martin's Hemi-powered 'Cuda. This photo (taken at Maple Grove in the early fall of 1970) is indicative of the next decade, where the scene was repeated almost weekly. (Photo Courtesy Carl Rubrecht)

Grumpy's Toy VI, shown here at York in the summer of 1970. The car was sold in 1972 and is now believed to be in the western Pennsylvania area. (Author Collection)

Chapter Four

eliminations. It's doubtful that even Bill knew it at the time, but this proved to be his last race behind the wheel of a Super Stocker.

At the *Car Craft* magazine awards banquet (held in conjunction with the Nationals), Bill walked away with awards for Stock Engine Builder, Super Stock Engine Builder, and Super Stock Driver.

Bill hadn't run an automatic transmission since the days of *Black Arrow*, but a Turbo-Hydramatic 400 was shipped to him (in pieces) from Chevrolet and tried in the Camaro, with little success. Because no high-stall torque convertors were yet available for the 400 transmission, it never performed to Bill's satisfaction.

Ed Hedrick's Super Stock Yenko Camaro was prepared by Jenkins. Ed recalls a Friday evening when Bill felt Ed's own Camaro was laying down in the top of first gear. He wanted to make some adjustments to

In his final days of SS/C racing, Jenkins held the class MPH record of 131.05, while Dave Strickler (in his Old Reliable *Camaro) held the ET record with a 10.74-second charge. This photo was captured at the Super Stock Nationals in the summer of 1969.* (Photo Courtesy Joel Naprstek)

The Strickler-Jenkins Clinic ran from mid 1968 through mid 1970, when Bill's involvement ended. The Grumpy's Toy VI *Pro Stocker is in the foreground.* (Photo Courtesy Michael "Mashie" Mihalko)

94 Grumpy's Toys

the carburetor; he felt the issue was caused by fuel starvation. While Bill worked on Ed's car, he suggested that Ed work on *Grumpy's Toy* and try to sort out the suspension, in an attempt to make the automatic transmission work better. So Ed began making adjustments and then tried them out by laying rosin across the 80 to 100 feet of Jenkins' shop floor, and then doing first-gear launches. You can just imagine the noise level as Ed made his full-throttle, first-gear blasts across the shop. Each launch ended with the Camaro sliding across the shop floor. Ed remembers clenching the wheel, fearful that he'd take out the oil pan on the lift at the end of the shop. Ed said, "We never did get the car to run any better, because the problem was with the converter. There simply was nothing available at that point."

With little to no success showing for their efforts, the automatic was pulled and later sent to Vitar for rebuilding. Early in 1970, the transmission was installed in Ed Hedrick's Camaro, along with a recently released 9-inch high-stall torque converter.

Ed was having little success with his Camaro in the SS/D class at this point, as the factory-backed, Hurst-built, American Motors AMX cars were dominating the class. Ed switched to SS/DA for the NHRA Gatornationals and captured the Super Stock crown, along with setting a new class record with an 11.28-second run. This proved to be the only Yenko Camaro to ever win a national event.

Outside of the occasional match race, *Grumpy's Toy* saw little action until the NHRA Springnationals

Ed Hedrick's SS/DA Yenko Camaro enjoys some serious bite at the NHRA Gatornationals in 1970. Jenkins' 525-hp 427-ci big-block powered the car to a new national record. (Ed Hedrick Collection)

Another shot of Ed Hedrick's Jenkins-prepared Yenko Camaro, this time in SS/E form. Ed sold the car after 1970, and, not long afterward, lost track of its whereabouts. Does anybody know what became of this missing Yenko car? (Ed Hedrick Collection)

in 1970, where it emerged to replace *Grumpy's Toy IV* in Pro Stock. Running the 430-ci Can-Am–based aluminum-block engine, Bill powered the Camaro to an off-pace 10.13-second time before falling victim to Lee Smith's Hemi 'Cuda.

By mid 1970, Bill was running **Grumpy's Toy VI** and showing less success for his efforts. The Mopar contingency had finally found a way to really make the Hemi come alive, thanks in large part to the newly designed, independent-runner tunnel-ram intake manifold. (Photo Courtesy Michael "Mashie" Mihalko)

With the completion of *Grumpy's Toy VIII*, the 1969 car was retired after the season-ending NHRA Supernationals.

Through November and December 1971, Bill used the Camaro as a test bed to evaluate different small-block combinations for the forthcoming Pro Stock Vega.

Jenkins' Pro Stock Camaro pairs off against John Archbault's **Hydrophobia** 1957 Chevrolet sedan delivery stocker, circa 1970. Maple Grove is the racetrack. (Photo Courtesy Carl Rubrecht)

In 1969, Dave Strickler ran a new Jenkins-prepared Z/28 Camaro. Initially the car ran SS/J with a 302-ci engine, and later as a SS/C car powered by a 427-ci big-block. (Photo Courtesy Carl Rubrecht)

Super Stockers: 1966–1969

Al Olster and his L-72-powered *One Step Beyond* Camaro at Maple Grove. One of the few ZL-1 engines prepared by Jenkins found its way between the fenders of this car. Al was credited with coining the phrase "Grumps Group," which was eventually seen on the rear of Al's car, Ed Hedrick's Yenko Camaro, and, briefly, Bill's own 1969 car. (Photo Courtesy Carl Rubrecht)

Bill fell victim to "Akron" Arlen Vanke in the first round of eliminations at the 1970 Super Stock Nationals in York. The pair's rivalry dated back to the Factory Experimental days of the early 1960s. (Photo Courtesy Michael "Mashie" Mihalko)

The Stricker-Jenkins Clinic semi-trailer supported three race cars on this busy day at the 1970 Super Stock Nationals in York. Up front is the 1970½ show car, and behind it is the 1969 Camaro and 1968 SS/RS version. (Pit Slide Series Archive/www.quartermilestones.com)

Chapter Five

The Pro Stocks: 1970-1983

1970 saw the turbulent 1960s finally put to bed. The dawning of the age of Aquarius was supposedly upon us and so to was NHRA's Super Season. Legions of Super Stock drivers jumped ship, preferring to instead run the no breakout rules of the new for 1970 Pro Stock category. To Bill, it proved to be a natural progression from Stock, Super Stock, and finally heads up Pro Stock. "It was something we pushed for, for a couple years that finally it came together after Indy."

Grumpy's Toy VII, 1970½ Camaro

With the 1970½ Pro Stock car under construction, *Grumpy's Toy VII* was "thrown together" for promotional purposes. It either made the rounds with the Strickler-Jenkins Car Clinic or sat at the local strips while the 1968 or 1969 cars were being raced. Though the factory 375-hp 402-ci big-block was replaced with a ZL-1, the car was never raced.

Grumpy's Toy VII was easily identifiable by its non-Rally Sport fascia, its close-to-stock-appearing stance, and the ZL-2 hood. Bill received the hood from the good folks at Chevrolet. While it was originally slated for production, Chevrolet only made a few of these hoods before canceling the idea for several reasons. Primary reasons were production delays brought on by a strike and the changing attitude toward performance that was taking place at the time. Before disposing of the hoods, Chevrolet's Paul

Prior sent one Bill's way. A fiberglass replica of the hood was laid up and temporarily used on *Grumpy's Toy VIII*.

With Bill's involvement in the Car Clinics ending in mid 1970, he no longer had a use for the Camaro. He returned the car (along with the ZL-1) to Ammon R. Smith where it was sold to unknown interests.

Grumpy's Toy VIII, 1970½ Camaro

After the fiasco of the Chrysler mini meet that had taken place prior to the NHRA Nationals in September 1969, the NHRA finally buckled to driver demands and created a professional heads-up category. Pro Super Stock (as it was briefly referred to) made its debut in February 1970 at the Winternationals in Pomona, California.

Grumpy's Toy VII **photographed in May of 1970 at York, Pennsylvania. The ZL-1 engine and the car were both returned to Ammon R. Smith.** (Photo Courtesy Tom Schiltz)

Dave Strickler, always the class act, with his SS/C 1969 Camaro and Clinic trailer. (Photo Courtesy Mike Strickler)

Chapter Five

When compared to what the Super Stock drivers had proposed back in 1968, the NHRA heads-up category differed very little. A minimum weight of 7 pounds per cubic inch was agreed upon, with a minimum car weight (minus the driver) of 2,700 pounds. All cars had to be American made and produced within the past three years. The engine could be no larger than 430 ci, and could be topped by a maximum of two 4-barrel carburetors. The engine had to be produced by the same company that manufactured the body. Any internal engine modifications were permitted, along with any transmission, rear end, or tire, as long as they fit the "stock" wheel well. Fiberglass fenders, hoods, hood scoops (no taller than 7 inches), and deck lids were also permitted.

Dick Whitman crawls behind the wheel during a tuning session. The front spoiler didn't last long. (Photo Courtesy Carl Rubrecht)

Here's Grumpy's Camaro, as it was thrown together for the Hot Rod magazine photo shoot. Though Bill insists it was Grumpy's Toy VII on the cover, that may not be true. (Bill Jenkins Collection)

The Pro Stocks: 1970–1983

A number of competitors had new cars built between the time the new category was announced and the Winternationals debut. But due to the delayed release of the new Camaro, Bill relied on his 1968 car to get the job done.

While in California, Bill took delivery of a "body in white" 1970-1/2 Camaro from the General Motors Camaro/Firebird production facility in Van Nuys. Prior to shipping the shell east, the body was chemically milled to remove excessive weight.

The latest *Toy* made its debut late in May at ATCO, New Jersey, where it ran a match race against the Sox & Martin Hemi 'Cuda. An aluminum-block 430-ci big-block (wearing open-chambered, cast-iron heads) powered the Camaro to its first loss in what would prove to be a long season for Da Grump.

It's the Orange County Pro Stock Championship in February of 1970, and the Grump tries on a set of zoomies. No advantage was realized—just as quickly as they arrived, off they came. (Photo Courtesy Pat Smith/www.turboracingphotos.com)

Another rare photo from the car's very first outing. Here, Jenkins incorporates the unique scoop layout that adorned the Hot Rod *magazine cover in July 1970.* (Photo Courtesy Carl Rubrecht)

Chapter Five

For Pro Stock class action, the 430-ci Can-Am engine was pulled from the Winternationals- and Gatornationals-winning Camaro. The drivetrain was completed by a Borg-Warner 4-speed and 5.13:1 gears in a 12-bolt rear housing.

Dave Strickler drove the new Camaro at the NHRA Indy Nationals in September 1970, losing out in the second round of eliminations due to a mechanical failure. Bill qualified *Grumpy's Toy VI* in the number-2 position with a 9.91-second

Though on a later date, this photo was also taken at Maple Grove. Note that the front chin spoiler has been trimmed. The rear spoiler didn't last much longer. Jenkins found that the car actually gained 2.5 mph of top speed without them. (Photo Courtesy Kevin Johnson)

Grumpy's Toy VIII seen hazing the tires off the line at Maple Grove during its maiden voyage. Note the slip-on wheelie bars. (Photo Courtesy Carl Rubrecht)

The Pro Stocks: 1970-1983

elapsed time, but bowed out in the first round when he snapped off the left rear wheel while heating the slicks.

Mid 1970 through 1971 brought some pretty lean times for Jenkins. Though he held a low qualifying position at Indy in both 1970 and 1971 with *Grumpy's Toy VI*, there were no major event wins to show for his efforts. *Grumpy's Toy VIII* was living off its sponsors, who at the time were paying $10,000 to $20,000 each to have their name on the car.

Dave again. The fiberglass ZL-2 hood didn't last. The scoop, in combination with the "Grump Lump" beneath it, exceeded the NHRA's 7-inch height limitation rule. (Photo Courtesy Bob Plumer)

Dave Strickler found track conditions at the 1971 NHRA Winternationals ideal. Here he is piloting *Grumpy's Toy VIII*, which proved to be no match for Chrysler's Hemi-powered cars. (Photo Courtesy Bob Plumer)

Chapter Five

Here's Dave Strickler driving **Grumpy's Toy VIII** *at the NHRA Winternationals, charging out of the hole. It didn't seem to matter who was driving the car; 1971 was a tough year.* (Photo Courtesy Jim Handy)

The Pro Stocks: 1970–1983

By mid 1970, the factory-backed Hemi Chryslers had finally caught up to and surpassed the performance levels of Bill's Camaros. His background in mechanical engineering, along with an obsessive attention to detail, was no match for corporate dollars and a room full of Chrysler engineers dedicated to beating this 5-foot, 4-inch pest from Pennsylvania.

At the 1970 Car Craft All Star Team Awards, Bill cleaned house, collecting the awards for Pro Stock Driver, Pro Stock Engine Builder, Super Stock Engine Builder, and Man of The Year.

The 1970½ car, which ran a lagging NHRA-legal best of 9.52 seconds in 1971, had its greatest success while match racing. Toward the end of the 1971 season, Bill dropped a 494-ci engine into the Camaro for a match race in West Palm Beach, Florida. Running against "Draino Dan" (as Bill jokingly referred to him) Don Nicholson, the Camaro turned a then-unheard of 9.26-second elapsed time. For a man who claimed to be making a lot of guesses when it came to the big-blocks, it was obvious he was making a lot of good guesses.

Grumpy's Toy VIII *made use of the very first pair of Cragar's spun-aluminum rims. This style of wheel soon became the standard in many drag racing classes.* (Photo Courtesy Carl Rubrecht)

Grumpy pairs off against Bill Stiles in his factory-backed 1968 Hemi-urged Barracuda. The rear spoiler on Jenkins' Camaro advertised Ammon R. Smith Auto Company. Through the deal, Bill received a break on a leased Chevelle Malibu. (Photo Courtesy Carl Rubrecht)

Grumpy's Toys 105

Chapter Five

Though it was in match race form, the 494-inch engine, derived from a bored-and-stroked 430-ci Can-Am block (4.4375-inch bore x 4.00-inch stroke) powered the 3,000-pound Camaro to the fastest time to date by a Pro Stocker.

Late in 1971, Bill released his first book, *Chevy Power Guide*, in conjunction with the Engeldrum Publishing Company. Within the 66-page book, Bill spilled the beans on all his go-fast speed secrets—the ones that used factory high-performance Chevrolet parts. A thorough in-depth look at engine blocks, cylinder heads, and everything in between informed readers on how to choose the best parts to suit their needs.

Originally pegged to be match raced in 1972, *Grumpy's Toy VIII* was instead leased to Funny Car ace Bruce "Mr. Clean" Larson (*USA-1*), who'd seen one too many fires from the inside of a fiberglass body. Bruce leased the Camaro late in 1971 and campaigned it until his own Pro Stock Vega was ready for competition in 1972.

The Mylar decals were peeled and the car was leased out once again, this time to Richie Zul, who eventually purchased the car from Bill in 1974. The Camaro ended up in the hands of Dennis Ferrara, who captured the NHRA Competition Eliminator Championship with it in 1977.

The car has been restored back to its former *Grumpy's Toy* status, though some controversy does surround the fact. Numerous people have wondered whether or not the correct car was actually restored. Adding fuel to the controversy, when the car arrived at Jenkins Competition for authentication, Jenkins said, "There was nothing left of the original car but the roof, quarter panels, and rockers." Richie Zul said that the car should have been brought to him, because all the changes made to the car at that point were either made by him or Dennis Ferrara. "There was nothing left of the Jenkins car," Zul concluded.

Some between-rounds tuning on the Can-Am 430-ci big-block, circa 1970. Note the angled 750-cfm Holley carbs and modified Weiand intake manifold. (Photo Courtesy Michael "Mashie" Mihalko)

In legal trim, Grumpy's Toy VIII just could not compete with Chrysler's Hemi cars. But in match race trim, it was a different story. By the fall of 1971, Grumpy and his "mountain motor" (494 ci) Camaro had them all covered. (Photo Courtesy Bob McClurg)

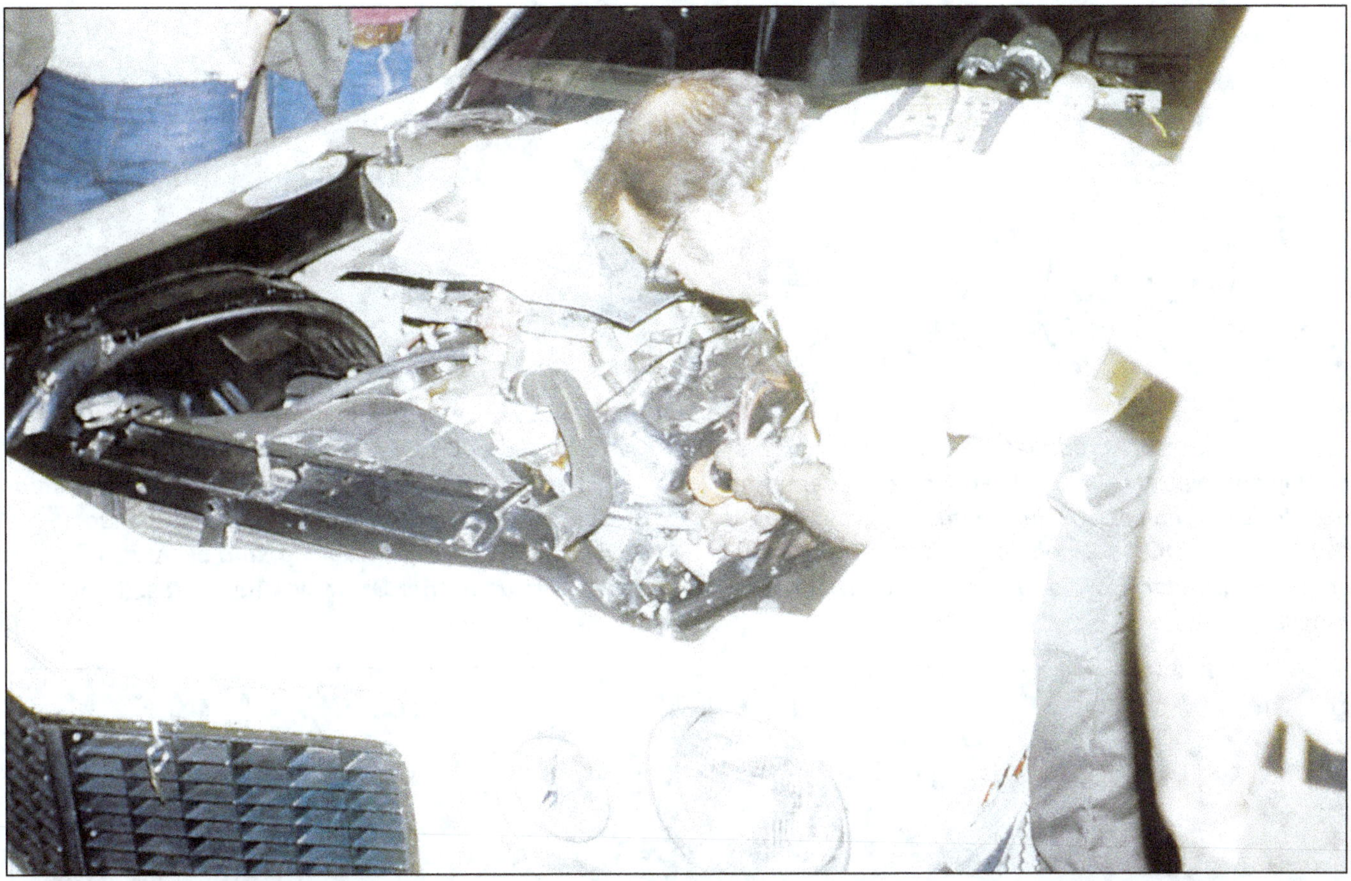

The Pro Stocks: 1970–1983

At the 1971 NHRA Nationals in Indianapolis, Indiana, Jenkins thrashed in vain on the big-block, bowing out early in eliminations. (Photo Courtesy Tom Kasch)

Bruce Larson, who had recently climbed out from behind the wheel of the USA-1 Camaro Funny Car, tried his hand at Pro Stock racing. The idle **Grumpy's Toy VIII** *was leased to Bruce, and was powered by a Jenkins-built cast-iron 427-ci big-block mill. Bruce campaigned the Camaro through 1972, until his own Pro Stock Vega was complete.* (Photo Courtesy Bob Plumer)

Chapter Five

Richie Zul, hard-pressed for a new race car after his freshly completed Camaro disappeared, became the next to lease the car. Richie eventually purchased the Camaro and ran sub-9-second ETs with a low-budget, cast-iron big-block for power. (Photo Courtesy Kevin Johnson)

Dennis Ferrara was the next driver for the race-weary Camaro. The car finally won some much-deserved glory when Dennis captured the World Championship with it before selling the car in 1978. It was discovered years later, bracket racing, and eventually restored to its former **Grumpy's Toy** status. (Photo Courtesy Bob Snyder)

Bill shares a laugh with Pittsburgh International Dragway tech director Jim Henderson, Ronnie Sox, and Buddy Martin during a 1971 match race session. Could it have been something about Sox's newfound power coming from a small-block Chevy? (Photo Courtesy Jim Henderson)

The Pro Stocks: 1970-1983

Grumpy's Toy IX, 1972 Vega

For the previous 18 months, Chrysler and its Hemi cars had run roughshod through Pro Stock. Excluding the 1971 NHRA Summernationals win by Don Nicholson, Chrysler had owned the category and, without some sort of intervention, the future appeared to hold more of the same. Something had to be done to breathe new life back into the category. Between Jack Hart (executive director of the NHRA) and Bill Jenkins, changes were on the horizon.

Due to the poor showing of his previous Pro Stock Camaro, Bill decided that, without new rules to level the playing field, he would just build a match race Chevy Vega for the 1972 season. Construction of the car began in the summer of 1971. Through the latter half of that year, Bill used *Grumpy's Toy VI*, a 1969 Camaro, to test various-displacement engines. Pairing the weight down to 2,850 pounds, he found using a 331- or a 350-ci engine, the car produced ETs in the 10.20s. Bill felt that if he could get the weight breaks he desired from the NHRA, it would make sense to run the smaller 331-inch engine.

It was in early December 1971 when Bill met with Jack Hart to hammer out new rules that would (hopefully) level the Pro Stock playing field. A conflict of interest you say? Maybe.

Knowing his small-block could be competitive in a lighter package, Bill pushed for NHRA approval of the short-wheelbase Vega. The idea was sold to Jack Hart from a marketing perspective—the buying public was purchasing smaller cars. By racing them, the crowds would pour in. The NHRA agreed, and new rules were written for the 1972 season. Chrysler representatives, sensing their domination in Pro Stock was being threatened, protested the new rules, but to no avail.

Reflecting back over 40 years, Bill regretted the new rules, saying, "It should never have been done." The category was meant to be heads-up and, in Bill's opinion, it took until the new rules in 1982 before things got back on track.

In New England for a WCS points meet, The Grump warms up the tires prior to a run against John Hagen and his Hemi 'Cuda. John built some of the nicest-looking Chrysler products, starting with his early 1968 Super Stock Barracuda. (Photo Courtesy Paul Wasilewski)

Chapter Five

In 1972, weight breaks were at the center of the new rules: Wedge-engine cars were required to carry 6.75 pounds per cubic inch; inclined-valve engines, 7.0 pounds per cube; and all others (specifically overhead-cam Fords and Chrysler's Hemi) were required to carry 7.25 pounds per cubic inch. Bill reflected, "Maybe the Chrysler people had upset Jack Hart or something; I don't know. But he didn't flinch when I presented the weight breaks to him."

Using the 331-ci small-block, Bill's Vega could weigh a minimum of 2,234 pounds. This was approximately 600 pounds less than the test Camaro that had been producing 10.20-second ETs. It would also be 800 pounds less than what the Hemi-powered cars would be required to carry.

Though Bill and his crew had started a Vega build over the summer, the car was scrapped. Bill said it had been "too cut up" to use once the new rules were in place. "We had been experimenting with different engines in different locations; under the cowl and behind the cowl." The building of the second Vega *(Grumpy's Toy IX)* began in December. Jenkins and crew put in 1,700 hours building it over the two months leading up to the Winternationals, to ensure it was ready for the first race of the new season.

The Pro Stock rules of the day required that the driver be protected from all angles and reinforced "step frames" were permitted. The Vega was a unibody design so Bill had Walt Weney and the folks at S-W Race Cars weld a step frame/roll cage for it. Jenkins' crew of Derrick Von Bargen and Dick Whitman, among others, performed the final assembly. Contrary to popular belief, *Grumpy's Toy IX* was not a full-tube-chassis car. The rocker panels on the stock Vega were key supports (frame rails, if you will) and Bill designed the 360-degree roll cage to tie into the inner rocker panels. The front suspension incorporated a Pinto steering rack, along with Roger Lamb–designed spindles and disc brakes. Beyond the steering components, the chassis was all Vega forward of the firewall.

Jenkins dominated Pro Stock in 1972 with his small-inch subcompact Vega. There was a mass exodus from pony cars that year; weight breaks had put the larger body style at a disadvantage. (Author Collection)

The Pro Stocks: 1970-1983

Because the Vega was manufactured with no true rear frame rails, a tubular subframe was added to the unibody to tie the roll cage and rear suspension together. Initially built with an adjustable four-link rear suspension, the car was updated with a three-link of Bill's design shortly after the Winternationals. The three-link's design was similar to the 1958 to 1964 Chevrolet full-size rear suspension. It incorporated a floating A-frame that tied the rear to the 4130 tubing. The rear end housing was an acid-dipped and drilled Dana 60 unit, carrying 5.57:1 gears.

The 331-inch small-block that propelled the Vega was derived from a .020-inch overbored 327. Bill said this was the first engine they built up based on what they'd accomplished on the newly installed Go Power dyno. "Unlike our previous engines, which we just put together and thought were good and then went out and tested, this one started on the dyno."

A high-mileage block was the starting point; Bill has always believed in using a "seasoned" block that had already settled and shifted. The cylinder block was tested for cylinder wall thickness with a sonic gauge. In a May 1972 article, *Car Craft* magazine reported that the first engine used in the Vega was the high-mileage, large-journal 327 that once powered Bill's tow rig. The 331 was topped by a pair of 292-casting "turbo" heads, featuring 2.06-inch-diameter intake valves. Initial preparation work was performed by Air Flow Research (AFR) in California.

The initial set of so-called turbo heads had been developed by Chevrolet's Ron Sperry in conjunction with Henry "Smokey" Yunick for use on a 209-ci turbocharged engine Smokey had prepared for the Indy 500. Though Chevrolet did have a strict "no racing" policy in place, Ron stated, "We wanted to ensure that those who did use our parts were successful."

Approximately 50 sets of these heads were cast for drag race use in the fall of 1971. This initial run of heads was modified from the original Smokey Yunick design and incorporated a conventional production combustion chamber design.

Ron Sperry noted that the initial 50 sets of cylinder heads were hard to work with; what you could do with them was limited. "You couldn't modify the heads to install large valvesprings without brazing or welding on them because you'd take the chance of running into water." The head was revised for over-the-counter sale in 1973, and featured improved intake and exhaust ports along with revised water jackets.

Bill warms the Firestone slicks as qualifying gets underway at the NHRA Summernationals. Suspension ills had plagued the Vega at the season-opening Winternationals, but were fixed with a rear-suspension redesign. (Photo Courtesy www.LesWelch.com)

Chapter Five

Jenkins completed his 331 with TRW pistons, featuring his own gas ports for better ring seal. Final compression was a healthy 13:1. A pair of Holley 660-cfm carburetors, perched on a heavily modified Edelbrock TR-1X tunnel ram manifold, completed the induction system. The little block initially produced a reported 540 hp at 7,500 rpm, and was what Ron Sperry referred to as "the start of Chevrolet's small-block development program."

Unlike many drivers, Bill only carried sponsors whose parts he used and believed in. For example, he worked closely with General Kinetics' Harold Brookshire in designing a camshaft that met his requirements. Camshafts became another part of Bill's expertise and, over the years, he spent numerous hours on design and development.

The transmission of choice was the trusted Borg-Warner 4-speed manual, running a 2.54 first gear, 1.68 second, and 1.31 third. The gears were all specially made using Borg-Warner tooling and were all good-quality nickel gears. From a size perspective, they were the largest gears you could fit in the iron case. To maintain the transmissions, of which Jenkins happened to have up to 28 "laying around" at the time, Bill hired one guy dedicated to building them and rebuilding them after every three or four runs. With pride, he states that he made approximately 250 runs in this car without missing a shift.

The Vega body was lightly dipped in acid to help remove unwanted weight. With the addition of fiberglass fenders, hood, and rear hatch, the body lost about 120 pounds. It was topped off with a stunning pearl-white paint job, with candy-apple red striping by Jim's Auto Body in Westchester, Pennsylvania.

The car was completed just a week before the Winternationals. Bill towed it across the country and made his first runs at Irwindale (not far from Pomona), hoping to dial the car in prior to heading to the Winternationals. Due to rear suspension issues that initially plagued the car, the Vega had problems running any quicker than 9.80-second ETs.

To the surprise of many, the Vega and its yards of tubing passed the Winternationals tech inspection. The only concern was the Hooker headers that exited from the lower fender. The problem was solved with a quick trip into town, where locally based Hooker bent up a new set of tubes that exited under the chassis.

As qualifying got underway, it was obvious that the rear suspension ills that had been causing handling issues had yet to be sorted out. The Vega qualified in the 17th spot with a not-too-impressive 9.90-second elapsed time. It appeared Chrysler's initial worries, regarding its class domination being threatened, were unfounded and it started the new season just as it had finished the last—in the winner's circle. The low qualifier of the event was Stu McDade in Billy Stepp's Dodge Challenger, who posted a 9.59-second elapsed time. Bill knew he had the horsepower to get around the Hemi-powered cars, but handling issues continued to plague the Vega throughout time trials.

As luck had it, the first round of eliminations paired Bill against top qualifier McDade. It was a race that surprised everyone. Grumpy took the lead with a holeshot and sent the Dodge packing with a 9.63-second run to a losing 9.75-second effort. Apparently, a cure had been found for the Vega's handling ills. Bill had essentially locked the rear end by adjusting the lower rear parallel links and also switching to Goodyear tires. These changes proved to be exactly what the car needed.

In the second round, Bill faced "The Red Light Bandit," Bill Bagshaw, and his Hemi-powered Dodge Demon. Bagshaw, with a reputation for cutting a mean light himself, was beaten by Jenkins at his own game. Bill launched first and finished first with a 9.62-second ET to a trailing 9.85-second pass. Could an upset be in the making? The Chevy fans, starved for a win, were beginning to get their hopes up.

Some drastic experimentation in cylinder head porting was taking place during the development of Chevrolet's Bowtie heads in the mid 1970s. Chevrolet engineer Ron Sperry referred to Bill as the father of the Bowtie cylinder head. (Bill Jenkins Collection)

The Pro Stocks: 1970–1983

In the semifinals, Bill faced Don Carlton in the Chrysler-backed *Motown Missile* 'Cuda. Off the line, Bill grabbed the lead on *Missile* and staved off Carlton's top end charge, running a 9.70 to Don's losing 9.84.

With the warm California sun fading in the distance, the final round was on and the estimated crowd of 55,000 spectators was on its feet to watch Jenkins face off against Don Grotheer. As *Car Craft* magazine reported, the two remaining cars lined up for the final go, and the suspension issues that had plagued the Vega earlier had returned. This threatened to create an unwanted upset for Jenkins and his fans. As the last amber bulb on the tree turned to green, Bill fought to keep the Vega straight and got the jump on Grotheer. Grotheer's catch-up effort was valiant but, on this day, the drag racing gods were favoring Bill. Shifting through the gears at 8,200 rpm, the Vega maintained the lead and downed the 'Cuda with a 9.68-second run at 140.18 mph to a losing 9.82-second pass at 141.95 mph. The crowd went nuts! Bill Jenkins and Chevrolet were back!

There was no denying it; Bill Jenkins was almost single-handedly responsible for breathing new life back into Pro Stock and making it a true professional category. His driving prowess was reminiscent of the 1965 Winternationals, where he'd taken Top Stock Eliminator by defeating each opponent on the starting line.

Almost immediately, customers wanted to place orders for an identical Vega. Jenkins' crew member, Derrick Von Bargen, left the Winternationals early and flew back to Pennsylvania to take a deposit on a new Vega from Carmen Rotunda. A new company called SRD (Speed Research & Development) Race Cars was formed immediately after the Winternationals, employing Jenkins' crew members Derrick Von Bargen, Dick Whitman, and Pete Hutchinson. Derrick recalled that by the time the Rotunda car was complete, they had a shop full of cars to build.

With *Grumpy's Toy IX* stripped down to its minimum weight of 2,000 pounds for match racing, it ran as quick as 9.19 through the quarter-mile. In legal NHRA trim, the Vega eventually ran a 9.35-second ET. Former Stock champ Larry Lombardo joined

And Pro Stock was never the same. Jenkins shocked the Winternationals crowd and set the competition on its ear, banging off 9.60 ETs. Note the one-time hood scoop and patchwork on the lower fender; the headers had initially exited here but the idea was rejected by NHRA tech. (Photo Courtesy Bob Plumer)

Chapter Five

the Jenkins Super Crew mid-summer and was groomed to be Bill's replacement behind the wheel. As he got older, Bill knew someone had to be able to drive his car better than he could. In the young Lombardo, he saw the skill and poise to handle the car without it going to his head. Lombardo made his first pass in the car late in the season, producing a 9.36-second time.

By season's end, the Vega (powered by a 354-inch small-block) produced 9.08-second times during tire test sessions. (Photo Courtesy www.LesWelch.com)

Few things bring a smile to the Grumpy one's face so quickly! Here, Bill accepts a Wally for his Summernationals win. (Photo Courtesy www.LesWelch.com)

The Pro Stocks: 1970-1983

Bill admitted spending $24,000 building the Vega, approximately three times the amount it had cost to build his first Pro Stocker. Over the Labor Day weekend, this investment paid dividends.

Bill bypassed the NHRA US Nationals at Indianapolis for the AHRA/PRA National Challenge held in Tulsa, Oklahoma. The National Challenge was organized by Don Garlits, who felt that the payouts given by the NHRA at its national events were inadequate. With the financial backing of AHRA president Jim Tice, the Professional Racers Association (PRA) held an alternate meet on Labor Day weekend, where the winner of each professional category received a guaranteed $35,000. This was the highest-paying event in drag racing history. By comparison, the average NHRA payout at the time was $4,000 to $5,000. Those who did attend Indy knew they at least had a chance of winning, because most of the big-name players were out of town.

Herb McCandless goes up while Jenkins goes on. Herb's wheelie bars failed, so Jenkins roared to a 9.46-second semi-final-round victory. (Photo Courtesy www.LesWelch.com)

At the NHRA Summernationals, Bill continued his steamrolling of Chrysler's Hemi-powered cars by defeating Dandy Dick Landy's Challenger with a 9.48-second pass at 144.23 mph. (Photo Courtesy Brian Beattie)

Grumpy's Toys 115

Chapter Five

Back in Tulsa, Pro Stock weight breaks were the talk of the day, with the Chrysler contingency threatening to boycott the race if organizers didn't lower the half-pound-per-cubic-inch weight difference between the Hemi-powered cars and the small-block Chevy-powered cars (which meant Grumpy Jenkins). A quarter-pound difference was finally agreed upon, and the threat of a Chrysler boycott was dropped. Jenkins marched on, and grabbed the low qualifying position, while Dick Landy's 16-plug Hemi Challenger held down the second spot. Less than .100 second separated the top five cars.

As reported in *Hot Rod* magazine at the time, Bill put away Gordon Collet's Hemi 'Cuda in round one, eliminated Don Grotheer in round two, and soloed in round three.

In the semifinals, Bill met West Coast legend Butch Leal and his Hemi-powered Duster. It was a close race; Bill nipped the Duster with a 9.39-second run at 146.57 mph to a losing 9.40-second blast at 146.10 mph.

In the final round, Bill met Herb McCandless and his Sox & Martin–sponsored Duster. The two cars staged evenly, and on the last yellow, Bill got a slight jump on McCandless and did not look back. On the top end, Bill took the win with a 9.46 at 145 mph to McCandless' 9.51 at 145.25 mph. With a total payout approaching $55,000, you can bet the Grump was smiling on that day.

At the NHRA World Finals in October, Bill defeated Ken Dondero in Don Nicholson's Ford to capture the Pro Stock Championship. Chrysler's initial fears proved correct—its domination of Pro Stock had come to an end.

At the season-ending NHRA Supernationals in November, Bill tried out a recently developed 354-inch small-block. It was essentially a .030-inch-overbored 350. Bill reported, at the time, that work on this engine had begun earlier in the season because it was unclear where the small car/small inch weight break may settle. Bill defeated Bob Glidden's Pinto in the first of Glidden's many final-round appearances. Though the Pinto ran a quicker time, Bill captured the win after getting the jump at the start line.

Jenkins' one major-event loss in 1972 was at the Gatornationals, where he fouled away his hopes in the semifinals. (Photo Courtesy Paul Wasilewski)

The Pro Stocks: 1970-1983

Essentially, the 354 was built for match racing and tire testing purposes. Jenkins could get 15 to 20 runs out of this "slow-turning engine" before having to freshen it up.

By the end of 1972, Bill had made his first million dollars, with the Vega contributing approximately $250,000 of the total. The little Vega had won six out of the seven national events in which it had been entered, capturing the NHRA Pro Stock title and earning Bill enough money to tie him with Wilt Chamberlain as the highest-paid sports figure in 1972.

At the annual *Car Craft* magazine awards banquet held in September, Bill walked away with the Pro Stock Engine Builder and Driver of the Year awards. *Super Stock & Drag Illustrated* magazine voted him Pro Stock Driver of the Year as well.

Prior to the Winternationals in January 1973, *Grumpy's Toy IX* was repainted red. This was Bill's first red car since the original *Grumpy's Toy* back in 1966.

Late in the winter, with Larry Lombardo driving, the Vega met up with Ronnie Sox for a match race at Sunshine Dragstrip in St. Petersburg, Florida. Sadly, during this race the car was destroyed in a rollover crash. Thankfully, there were no injuries, but the car that revolutionized Pro Stock was a write off. Some felt red cars and Grumpy Jenkins just didn't mix, and maybe they were right. Maybe Bill felt the same way; this was the last of his red race cars. When asked why he had switched to the red paint in the first place, Bill simply stated that it photographed better.

What didn't Jenkins win in 1972? The NHRA Northeast Division Man of the Year award was another of his trophys. His first National-event-win trophy is still the one he is most proud of. (Photo Courtesy Mike Goyda)

Neither the red paint nor the car lasted for long. Grumpy's Toy IX is seen here at the NHRA Winternationals in 1973, wearing Wynns Oil as its latest sponsor, a deal that lasted through 1975. (Photo Courtesy Bob Plumer)

Chapter Five

After the 1969 season, Bill found little time for outside customers anymore; maintaining his own Pro Stock cars required his undivided attention. Wallace & Silman campaigned one of Grumpy's old Camaros in B/MP (seen here at the NHRA US Nationals in 1972). It was one of the few cars prepared by Jenkins Competition in the 1970s. (Photo Courtesy www.LesWelch.com)

Grumpy's Toy X, 1972 Vega

How popular was Bill Jenkins? In 1973, *The Wall Street Journal* and *TIME* magazine carried articles enlightening the outside world on the highest-paid sports figure of 1972. *TIME* gave a brief history of the man they referred to as "Grumpy the Drag King" and included a breakdown of his earnings based on his trips down the racetrack. It was calculated that Bill was pulling in $5,650 per minute.

Driven by an inflated ego brought on by his celebrity status, Bill was truly living the life of a rock star. There were stories of the occasional trashed hotel room and his predilection for the company of the opposite sex. If you happened to have purchased the October 1973 issue of *Hot Rod* magazine, you

Jenkins and the freshly painted Vega pair off against the Plymouth Duster of Sox & Martin during the AHRA Winternationals, held at Beeline Dragway in 1973. (Photo Courtesy Steve Reyes)

The Pro Stocks: 1970–1983

Terry Cook went where no car magazine editor had gone before, and hopefully will never go again. "I suggested it, and Bill said, 'Sure.' He has a good sense of humor and found amusement in it all." (Author Collection)

The white car and an unimpressed-looking Mr. Jenkins. The Vega, brought into service early, was raced just once in this plain white wrapper, here at the NHRA Gatornationals. (Photo Courtesy Tom Kasch)

Outwardly, there is little difference in the 1973 car. Under the skin, however, a redesign of the chassis saved a few pounds along with gaining additional underhood space. This allowed for a variety of engine and transmission combinations. (Author Collection)

would have seen a very colorful center-spread of Mr. Jenkins. It was not the latest version of *Grumpy's Toy*—it was Bill. There, in most of his splendor, was Mr. Jenkins. He was laid out on a bearskin rug wearing nothing but boxers, a pair of sneakers, and a cigar-filled grin. This was not exactly what the *Hot Rod* demographic wanted to see, but, in that one shot, Terry Cook did capture the essence of Bill's sense of humor.

Cook said, "Bill and I had a pretty good rapport then, and this was around the same time that *Playgirl* magazine appeared on the newsstand with its Burt Reynolds center-spread. We thought a spin on the Burt Reynolds thing would be hilarious, so I asked Bill and he agreed."

To top off the accolades, Bill was the recipient of *Car Craft* magazine's coveted Ollie award in 1973, for his ongoing contributions to the sport of drag racing. Could it get any better than this for the one they called Grumpy?

Grumpy's Toy X made its debut in March at the Gatornationals in Florida. The Vega was brought into action earlier than expected, due to the crash of *Grumpy's Toy IX*. Early photos of the new car show it void of the red side stripes.

The new Vega was built in-house with former S-W Race Cars' employee Ed Quay welding up the chassis. Changes to the new car included additional width between the underlying tubing, allowing the use of the Lenco clutchless 4-speed transmission. This was something many of the top drivers were using by the end of the Winternationals in 1973.

The stock Vega radiator support and inner fenders were replaced by bent tubing and aluminum paneling, freeing up room for a big-block, should the need arise. In total, the new Vega realized a weight savings of about 120 pounds over the previous car.

Bill made the switch to the Lenco transmission after the Gatornationals in March. Though he felt there was only minimal improvement in elapsed

The Summernationals winners pose for posterity with their much-deserved Wallys. In the top row, from left to right, are: Jeb Allen, Don Schumacher, and Bill Jenkins. In the bottom row, from left to right, are: Lorry Azevedo, Bob Riffle, Larry Nelson, and Truman Fields. (Photo Courtesy www.LesWelch.com)

The Pro Stocks: 1970-1983

time, he praised the $2,700 Lenco because it minimized shock to the drivetrain and thus reduced parts breakage.

The NHRA revised the Pro Stock weight breaks for 1973, and ended up favoring the Ford's Cleveland engine, causing the Grump to lose a bit of advantage. The canted-valve Cleveland, with its superior breathing capabilities, could be stuffed in a Pinto and run at the same weight as the small-block Vega. Bill's current rendition of the 331-ci small-block was producing upwards of 600 hp—barely adequate against the Ford.

Though he was eliminated early at the NHRA Winternationals, while running the 1972 car, Bill set the new MPH record at 148.76. Both the MPH and ET records were tossed back and forth between Bill and the Fords throughout the year. And as predicted by many, the Ford of Gapp & Roush won the Pro Stock Championship at the end of the season.

In August, while in St. Louis for the AHRA Gateway Nationals, Bill's ramp truck and record-setting Vega were stolen. As reported in *Drag Racing USA* at the time, Bill rolled into town and qualified at number-1 with an impressive 8.97-second performance at 153.05 mph (which were new AHRA records). He and his crew loaded the car back onto the truck and headed out of town for an evening match race against Herb McCandless. Satisfied with defeating Herb three straight, the team rented hotel rooms in town for the night, planning to head back to St. Louis the following morning. After stopping for a late breakfast in Collinsville, Illinois, they returned to the parking spot where they had left the truck and it was gone. *Grumpy's Toy X* had made the growing list of stolen race cars. *The Hawaiian* Funny Car, *Hedman Hustler* Pro Stock Maverick, and Richie Zul's Pro Stock Camaro had all previously disappeared.

The police were contacted and a search was launched. Back at the St. Louis International Raceway, an announcement went out over the PA system, notifying the crowd of what had happened, and requesting any witnesses to come forward. Many folks claimed to have seen the car, but all initial tips led nowhere. By mid-afternoon, an anonymous call led to the retrieval of the ramp truck, but there was still no car.

In a complete turnaround of 1972, Bill's only national event win in 1973 was against Butch Leal at the NHRA Summernationals. (Photo Courtesy Steve Reyes)

Chapter Five

Grumpy's Toy X at Keystone, circa 1973. The car was later updated with a 1974 Vega front clip and taillights. Jenkins admitted seeing no advantage in the "swoopier-looking" 1974 Vega front clip. (Photo Courtesy Bill Truby)

It's Ford versus Chevy in a battle of the small-block-powered subcompacts. Chrysler, having no legal subcompact to campaign, boycotted what it considered an unfair added weight requirement placed on its Hemi cars. (Photo Courtesy Bob McClurg)

The state of Pro Stock tow rigs in 1973. The flatbed disappeared as enclosed trucks gained popularity due to the added security they offered. They also protected the increasingly valuable race cars from the elements. (Photo Courtesy John Johnson)

The following day, the police followed up a previous lead and searched an isolated old farmhouse in Centerville. There, in the garage, was the abandoned Vega. Ed Quay (a team member on the trip) said it was hard to believe, but whoever stole the car had only taken the engine, transmission, and the aluminum motor mounting plates. "They took the car apart with the same care we would have. They had destroyed nothing, and the only real problem was that they had taken the motor plates, which at the time, we didn't have duplicates of."

Ed also said that the fun part began as soon as the car was found. At the time, Jenkins was racing four to five times each week, either with the United States Racing Team or at booked-in match races. The car was found on a Sunday and Jenkins had planned to circuit race in Epping, New Hampshire, the following Wednesday night. The car was loaded back onto Bill's C-10 ramp truck and driven the 16 hours back to Malvern, Pennsylvania, where work to put the car back together started immediately. The whole crew chipped in, installing a fresh engine and transmission. By Tuesday afternoon, the car was ready for Wednesday's race in Epping.

Jenkins and his crew had some fun at the other racer's expense. They talked up the story of the car being stolen and all the good parts being taken, thus convincing the other racers that they would be running their back-up motor. Their first-round opponent was Maskin & Kanners' AMC Hornet. Believing the story, Kanners waited for a solid green before leaving the line—big mistake. Jenkins

The Pro Stocks: 1970–1983

Lombardo looks on as Jenkins makes necessary adjustments to the 660-cfm Holley center-squirt carburetors. Note the heavily reworked Edelbrock TR-1Y manifold. This intake's plenum has been re-shaped and reduced in size by about 50 percent, along with modifications to the runner length and volume. (Photo Courtesy Michael "Mashie" Mihalko)

In September, Bill captured both ends of the national record, running an 8.91-second pass at 154.37 mph during a WCS points meet at ATCO Raceway in New Jersey. Seen here at Ohio's Dragway 42, the Vega bounced the record back and forth all season with the Fords of Bob Glidden, Dyno Don Nicholson, and Gapp & Roush. (Author Collection)

defeated Kanners, laying down a stunning 8.90-second elapsed time.

The 1973 National Challenge was held the weekend prior to the NHRA Indy Nationals, giving drivers the opportunity to attend both races. The payouts were down at that year's PRA race; the winner in each category would receive $25,000. Unlike 1972, this included contingency money.

Bill returned as the defending Champion and qualified in fourth position, with a 9.166-second time. Of the 32-car Pro Stock field, Butch Leal held the low qualifying position with a 9.077-second run.

Butch Leal, known as "The California Flash," and his Hemi-powered Plymouth Duster faced off against Bill in the final. Both cars had been running like clockwork, banging off 9.10 elapsed times, and a close race was expected. The eager crowd was not disappointed. Leaving the line together, it was a race to the finish with Bill nipping the Duster on the top end with a 9.081-second

Grumpy's Toys 123

Chapter Five

run at 150.00 mph to Butch's losing 9.169-second effort at 149.75 mph.

The Vega was retired from NHRA competition after its 1974 Winternationals defeat of Gapp & Roush's Pinto. In one of the closest Pro Stock races to date, Bill downed Wayne Gapp with an 8.93-second pass at 152.54 mph to a losing 8.94-second run at 152.02 mph. Shortly afterward, the car was updated with a 1974 Vega front clip and taillights, and it was run on the AHRA circuit by the recently hired Ken Dondero.

In 1973, the Pro Stock category was overrun with Chevrolet Vegas. It seemed that wherever Grump went, the Chevrolet fraternity was sure to follow. (Photo Courtesy John Johnson)

*Match racing was all the rage in the mid 1970s, and Jenkins drew most of his income running against the likes of Ronnie Sox. Jenkins is seen here at Pittsburgh International Dragway in the updated **Grumpy's Toy X**, running against the Sox & Martin Hemi-powered Dodge Colt.* (Photo Courtesy Bill Truby)

The Pro Stocks: 1970-1983

The United States Racing Team was formed by Al Carpenter in 1971, and consisted of some of the biggest names in Pro Stock racing. The idea was to promote the cars and drivers, raise awareness, and hopefully gain some sponsorship cash to help ease the financial burden car owners were facing. About a dozen circuit races were run each year, but, by 1974, the team had lost momentum and finally disbanded. Bill can be seen in the lower left of this 1973 team photo. (Bill Jenkins Collection)

Ken was coming off a couple very satisfying seasons driving for Dyno Don Nicholson. But due in part to the fuel crisis that was affecting America at the time, Don was looking to cut back his operations and suggested to Ken that he take up Bill's offer to drive.

Bill hired Ken with the idea of running two cars for the season. At the time, Bill was doing most of the driving because Larry Lombardo had shaken his confidence with the crash of the 1972 car. Ken's hiring caused a little friction in the Jenkins camp and, within a few months, things boiled over. Ken finally

Bill had two cars at Englishtown in March 1974, making for an eight-car match race. Here, Ken Dondero catches some air while piloting Grumpy's Toy X *at that race.* (Photo Courtesy Steve Bell)

Chapter Five

had enough of the continuous bickering, and came to an agreement with Bill: He would run the AHRA races with crew member Dave Christie and Bill, using the new Vega, would run the NHRA races with Larry.

Ken's first outing with the Vega was at the World Finals held at Orange County International Raceway (OCIR) in March. He won the event; he defeated Lee Hunter with an 8.96-second blast at 153 mph to a losing 8.97-second pass at 151 mph. Ken's ET and MPH were both new AHRA records. Ken went on to win the AHRA Pro Stock Championship in 1975, running first in the Vega, and then made the switch to *Grumpy's Toy XII* late in the season.

As with the NHRA car, the token 331-ci small-block was used for class racing while the 354-ci mill was used for match racing. Ken recalled that "Bill

Ken Dondero piloting **Grumpy's Toy X**. Other than crowd appeal, Bill found no advantage in the 1974 sheetmetal when test runs compared it to the less-aerodynamic-looking 1973 sheetmetal. (Photo Courtesy Pat Smith/www.turboracingphotos.com)

With NHRA weight breaks favoring Ford teams in 1973, Jenkins earned only one major event win. If it was any consolation, his was the only Chevy to win any national event that year. (Photo Courtesy Bob Plumer)

The Pro Stocks: 1970–1983

always took the first four good engines to run the NHRA with, and I would get engine number-5 and whatever was left. Bill would jokingly say, 'You don't think I'd give you the good stuff,' but even Jenkins' fifth engine was better than most team's number-1 engine." Using the 331, Ken drove the Vega to a best time of 8.59 seconds at 159 mph.

The Vega was sold in late 1975 to fellow racer Jack Trost, who had minimal success running the car before parting with it. The car was last known to be running brackets in Pennsylvania.

In a move slightly off the beaten path for Jenkins, he was commissioned by Vince Piggins of Chevrolet to develop a 358-inch small-block for NASCAR competition. With the onslaught of the fuel crisis in 1974, NASCAR did its part to conserve fuel by lowering its maximum cubic-inch limit from its then-current 366-inch point. Former Rookie of the Year, Donnie Allison, and his DiGard Racing Chevrolet Laguna ran a Jenkins Competition–built 358 in 1974 and 1975. He went on to hold pole position at the Daytona 500 and the Firecracker 400 in 1975, and finish a best of third at Darlington. Jenkins said that Vince's interest in NASCAR was fleeting and, in no time, something else piqued his interest and he moved on.

Though fellow drag racers Dick Landy and Billy Stepp had each previously attempted to make use of existing dry sump technology, it wasn't until late 1973 that Bill perfected a system specifically for drag race use.

Simply, a dry sump oil system uses an external tank to store the oil away from the rotating crankshaft assembly, thus freeing up horsepower. Two pumps are incorporated: one to pump oil into the engine from the storage tank, and another to extract

The not-so-Grumpy one shares a rare trackside laugh with Billy "The Kid" Stepp in 1973. (Photo Courtesy Bill Truby)

Ken Dondero does his impression of a smoky funny car burnout in Grumpy's Toy X, *shown here at Pittsburgh International Dragway during the late winter of 1975. Ken spent two years with Jenkins, and though he ran the occasional NHRA race, he called the AHRA home. He won the AHRA Championship in 1975 and 1976.* (Photo Courtesy Bill Truby)

Chapter Five

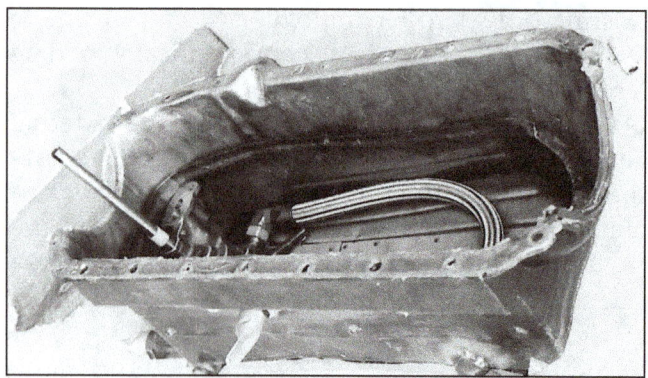
Through extensive testing, Jenkins discovered that a deep sump oil pan was the key to making horsepower with the dry sump system. At full throttle, the pan is near empty. (Photo Courtesy Larry Schreib)

*The well-worn **Grumpy's Toy X** was finally retired in 1975. The car had previously been updated with the 1974 front clip and taillights, and can easily be distinguished from **Grumpy's Toy XI** by its body-hugging bumpers.* (Photo Courtesy Bill Truby)

A Weaver Brothers three-stage belt-driven pump was the heart of the dry sump system. The front two sections scavenged oil from the baffled pan, while the third stage fed pressurized oil to the firewall-mounted filter, and on through the engine. (Photo Courtesy Larry Schreib)

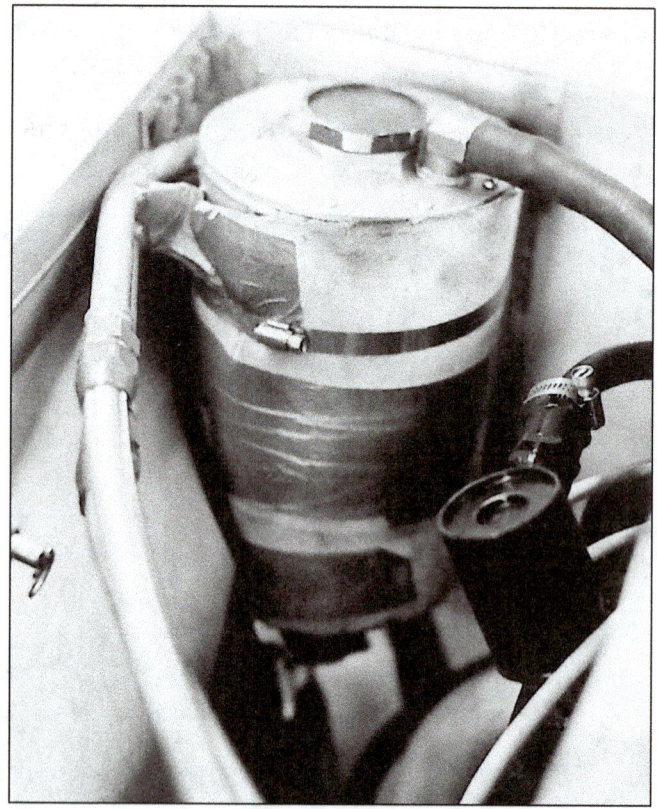
The reservoir for the dry sump held 4 quarts of Pennzoil's finest, while the complete system held approximately 8 quarts. The top hose is for crankcase ventilation. (Photo Courtesy Larry Schreib)

or scavenge oil from the engine. Bill made use of a Weaver Brothers belt-driven pump to do the job. In his book *The Chevrolet Racing Engine,* Bill stated that countless hours had been spent on pan development. But once they realized you didn't need a shallow pan (as did most dry sump systems), they were on their way.

Making use of the dry sump setup, Jenkins saw an approximate 30-hp increase over the traditional wet sump system.

Because dry sumps used an external oil tank, it allowed for a shallower-than-normal oil pan, which enabled a lower-profile car, thus improving aerodynamics. This was something Bill looked for in his next *Toy.*

In 1973, Jenkins Competition relocated. It was moved a couple doors up the road to a modern 6,000-square-foot building, which Bill had designed and built to his own plans. With a certain level of pride, Bill stated that the money he had earned match racing between 1968 and 1973 covered the cost of erecting the new building. To this day, Jenkins Competition remains at this location.

Grumpy's Toy XI, 1974 Vega

In later years, Bill downplayed the significance of *Grumpy's Toy XI*. But in 1974 the car was, by far, the most innovative Pro Stock race car to date. What made this car unique was its full-tube chassis, the MacPherson strut front suspension, the rack-and-pinion steering, and its dry sump oiling system. Not only were each of these innovations Pro Stock firsts, they remained staples in the sport for the next 35 years, and counting.

Unlike the previous two Vegas, *Grumpy's Toy XI* was a true full-tube-chassis car, bent by SRD to Bill's own specifications. The new chassis extended through the fabricated firewall, incorporating a MacPherson strut suspension, thus eliminating the last of the stock Vega underpinnings. The suspension was designed by the folks at Jenkins Competition in conjunction with SRD and Roger Lamb of Lamb Components. While skimming through a magazine one evening, Jenkins employee Ed Quay spotted an advertisement for a car that incorporated the suspension design and thought it was exactly

Jenkins catches some air coming off the line at Numidia Dragway. (Photo Courtesy Harold Hoch)

Chapter Five

what they needed to free up room in the new car. "We always had problems in the Vegas with the A-arm front suspension—trying to gain enough room for the headers to exit the head without a quick turn."

Roger Lamb said, "Bill invited me to come East. They had a fresh idea for a strut suspension. The idea was to get the car down out of the air and open up the engine compartment." Roger laid up the plans

The near-complete skeleton of Grumpy's Toy XI *is laid up on the chassis jig at Speed Research and Development (SRD). The total weight of the completed chassis was a shade over 100 pounds. Note the high front-strut mount, the first of its kind, designed by Bill Jenkins in conjunction with Roger Lamb and Dick Whitman. It was changed on later cars to allow for a lower profile.* (Photo Courtesy Pete Hutchinson)

The Pro Stock chassis, as designed by Bill Jenkins and Dick Whitman, has not changed much over the years. This same basic layout remains a staple in Pro Stock racing to this day. The rear motor plate and mounts can be seen here. (Photo Courtesy Pete Hutchinson)

To see the plus side of 150 mph, Bill felt the car had to be close to the ground. The MacPherson strut suspension and dry sump oil pan made this possible. Header clearance was close to 3 inches. (Photo Courtesy Bill Truby)

The Pro Stocks: 1970–1983

Shown here are the rear coil-over shock mounts and the frame mount for the Vega's three-link rear suspension setup. It features multiple anchor points for fine tuning. (Photo Courtesy Pete Hutchinson)

A head-on view of the nearly complete chassis. Motor plates were designed for the small-block and big-block applications. (Photo Courtesy Pete Hutchinson)

The car is slowly coming together. The SRD crew built an average of six to eight cars per year during its heyday, and about 95 percent of them were drag race cars. The dashboard was fiberglass and housed switches for fuel and ignition, along with the fuse panel. (Photo Courtesy Pete Hutchinson)

With the acid-dipped body in place, final fit and finish can be carried out. The wheel tubs were fabricated from lightweight aluminum and the 4130 chrome-moly tubing was Tig or heliarc welded. (Photo Courtesy Pete Hutchinson)

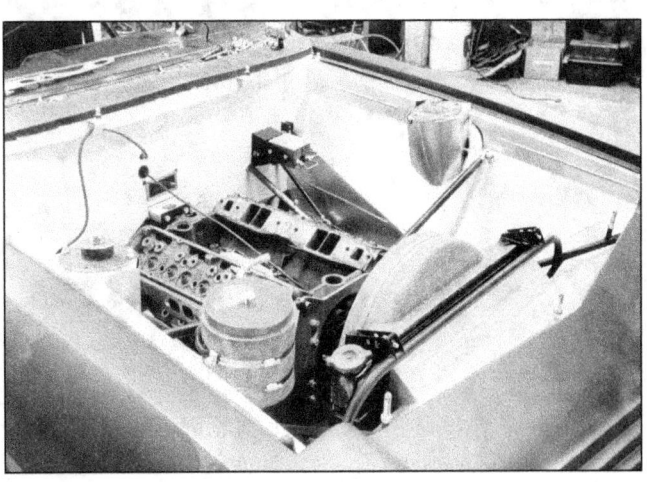

Here's a good look at the nearly complete Vega engine bay. Note the high struts and the mysterious window in the firewall. The stock Vega radiator actually proved to be adequate for quarter-mile jaunts. (Photo Courtesy Pete Hutchinson)

Grumpy's Toys 131

on paper and, once given the dimensions (top mount, center line, etc.), he went to work.

The fabricated uprights were bolted to a set of Lamb-designed struts, which were loosely based upon Datsun 240Z units but at only one third of the weight.

The strut dictated the general layout and, for geometry purposes, the spindle was at the strut centerline with a very high upper strut mount. The struts bolted to the upper chassis tube, which doubled as the engine mount. The struts were so high that the hood had to be notched for clearance. At that point, Roger knew they had to do something else, so they redesigned the setup in 1976. The finished suspension included a basic Pinto rack-and-pinion steering setup, fabricated tubular lower control arms, and 1/8-inch steel cables incorporated to limit suspension travel. The new chassis and strut suspension cut about 150 pounds of weight off the new car.

To compensate for driver weight, the Lenco transmission and Dana rear axle were offset 1 inch to the passenger side of the car.

The Lenco 4-speed, now Pro Stock standard equipment, carried a 2.95 first gear, while the Dana rear end (40 inches across) housed 6.17:1 gears. Jenkins' own three-link rear suspension, with its 48 positioning holes, supported the rear end.

The body was shipped to California to be acid-dipped. At the time, it was the only place a racer could get it done. The lightened body was strengthened in strategic places with expandable foam. Fiberglass bumpers, rear hatch, and hood were hung on the body and then fellow racer Jack Trost painted it ermine white.

With Chrysler's ongoing boycott of NHRA's Pro Stock category (due to what it felt was an unfair weight break of 7 pounds per cubic inch for the Hemi), the category became more of a Chevrolet vs. Ford battle. The superior Cleveland-headed Fords (the odds-on favorite at any national event) ran the same 6.65 pounds per inch as the small-block Chevrolet.

At the 1975 Springnationals, Jenkins defeated Roy Hill's Plymouth Duster with an 8.98-second run to a losing 9.16. This was Bill's record-setting 11th Pro Stock national-event win. (Photo Courtesy Thomas Nagy)

Jenkins brought his trick new Vega to the NHRA Springnationals, but was shut out by eventual winner Wayne Gapp. (Photo Courtesy Thomas Nagy)

The Pro Stocks: 1970–1983

Jenkins introduced the Vega in March at ATCO Raceway during a match race against the Ford of Gapp & Roush. This was a rematch of sorts to their Pomona race, where Gapp had laid a holeshot on Jenkins, defeating him with an 8.97-second run to a quicker-but-losing 8.87-second effort. This time, Jenkins and the new Vega defeated the Pinto in three straight runs, turning a best of 8.86 at 152 mph to Gapp's losing best of 8.92 seconds at 152 mph.

The completed Vega, seen at York in 1974, raised the bar for how future Pro Stock race cars should be designed and built. (Photo Courtesy Bill Truby)

*Bill in **Grumpy's Toy XI** at Englishtown, New Jersey, in March 1974. Note the new-design hood scoop.* (Photo Courtesy Steve Bell)

Chapter Five

For the third straight year, Jenkins and company won the NHRA Summernationals. With Larry Lombardo behind the wheel, the Vega defeated Scott Shafiroff, Bob Glidden, and Dave Kanners (in his AMC Hornet X) before meeting the new Gapp & Roush four-door Maverick in the final round. In one of the most satisfying races of his career, Lombardo strapped a holeshot lead on Gapp that he couldn't make up. The Vega tripped the lights with a 9.11-second pass at 150 mph (even), to Gapp's quicker (but losing) 9.02-second run at 151.77 mph.

Don Garlits organized another National Challenge drag race in 1974. Jenkins, having won the previous two, attended with hopes of making it a three-peat. The Professional Racers Organization (as they were now referred to) held the race at the New York Speedway. Just as the previous year's National Challenge, the race was held the weekend prior to the NHRA Nationals. Though the $15,000 win money (which now included contingencies) was down from the previous year's payouts, it was still close to double what the NHRA was paying for a professional category win at the Nationals.

In a blow-by-blow dissection of the event, *Super Stock & Drag Illustrated* magazine concluded that the race would go down as one of the worst in history due to poor organization, an inadequate field of cars, bad weather, and poor attendance. The Pro Stock field, which generally ran 32 cars, had to make do with the 23 that showed up for the event. All of the Pro Stockers ran at the same 6.75 pounds per cubic inch and, though one would think that this would favor the Chrysler Hemi contingency, the racing proved differently. Jenkins qualified his Vega at .100 second quicker than the fastest Hemi-powered car.

Bill put away the Mopars of Ronnie Sox and Don Carlton, and the Ford of Gapp & Roush on his way to the finals, where he defeated Mike Fons' hard-charging *Motown Missile* Hemi 'Cuda. Bill banged off times of 8.81, 8.79, 8.78, and 8.80 seconds at speeds in excess of 155 mph. Bob Glidden, driving a Cleveland-powered Pinto, captured the first of his many NHRA Pro Stock titles in 1974. Regardless of Glidden's Championship, *Car Craft* readers showed their bias and voted Bill Jenkins the Pro Stock Driver of the Year once again.

Jenkins' Vega won two NHRA national events in 1974. This is notable because it was the only Chevy to win a national event in 1974. His quickest legal time turned that year was an 8.74-second pass at 154 mph.

Hoping for every advantage possible, Jenkins started to conduct extensive aerodynamics studies on the new-for-1975 Chevrolet Monza hatchback body. Though Chevrolet officially introduced the

"Everyone Loves a Winner" the Vega advertisement read. While the marketers probably didn't have the NHRA Pro Stock class in mind when they wrote it, Bill Jenkins sure did when he read it. While the 15-inch slicks got the Vega down the track in a hurry, the parachute was needed to stop the car from 150-plus mph. (Photo Courtesy Bill Truby)

Monza in September 1974, Jenkins didn't have his car ready for the track until August 1975. In the meantime, Bill collected his last national event win as a driver at the NHRA Springnationals in 1975. He defeated Roy Hill in his Petty-prepared Plymouth Duster, with an 8.98-second run at 152.28 mph to Roy's 9.16-second pass at 149 mph.

The last race for the well-worn Vega was at the 1975 NHRA Summernationals. In a 2005 *Hemmings Motor News* article, Bill recalled selling the vehicle to Harold McCready immediately following the race. Harold removed the *Grumpy's Toy* decals and ran the

Relentless design and engine development included extensive modification of Edelbrock's TR-1X manifold. Countless hours were spent in the mid 1970s, optimizing intake runner length, along with plenum volume and shape. (Bill Jenkins Collection)

This 1974 photo shows another short runner design, this one incorporating a cast-iron base. (Bill Jenkins Collection)

Pittsburgh International Dragway was the location of this 1974 Pro Stock showing. Left to right: Fast Eddie Schartman, Dyno Don, Brooklyn Heavy, Grumpy's Toy, Don Carlton, and Maskin & Kanners' Hornet X. (Photo Courtesy Bill Truby)

Chapter Five

car with a 302-ci small-block for the next few seasons. "I just horsed around with it," McCready was quoted to say, "I never ran it in Pro Stock, as I just had too many things going on." It was restored by Glen Sharp and sold through Barrett-Jackson Auctions in 2007 for $525,000.

Grumpy's Toy XII, 1975 Monza

The new year started off with Mr. Jenkins wearing a suit and tie, peering out at us from the cover of *Car Craft* magazine. This was the first time any automotive magazine had featured a cover without a car present. It also removed any doubts of Bill's ongoing popularity.

The Monza was introduced in September 1975. It was built around the 97-inch-wheelbase H-Body platform and featured a body that was aerodynamically superior to the Vega that it eventually replaced. In building the new car, Bill felt the slippery Monza would be worth 3 to 4 mph over the Vega. This was Jenkins' first panel car, where each body panel was purchased separately, acid dipped in Jenkins' own vat, and then assembled over the SRD tube structure.

Don Prudhomme and Bill discuss the new SRD-built Monza while at the PHR Championship race in 1975. Since he was having no problem getting sponsors at this stage in his career, Bill noted that sponsors practically paid for the entire car. (Photo Courtesy Thomas Nagy)

Ronnie Sox and his Hemi Colt are seen here doing battle at York US-30. Grumpy's Vegas could be seen match racing like crazy throughout 1974 and 1975, powered by a slow-turning 354 and posting mid-8-second times. On any given weekend throughout the summer, either one of Bill's two Vegas could be seen running against the likes of Sox, Nicholson, Shafiroff, and Gapp & Roush. (Photo Courtesy Bill Truby)

The Pro Stocks: 1970–1983

Maintaining two cars in 1975 meant full-time work for up to 11 people. Bill oversaw it all himself, from parts ordering and development through payroll. (Photo Courtesy Larry Schreib)

Here's a look inside the heart of Grumpy's Toy XII. Bill stated that there was very little trickiness or mystery involved in building a small-block Chevrolet engine. However, he did not specifically say this about his own engines. Team Jenkins spent countless hours on design, development, testing, and evaluation, producing the power gains necessary to ensure each Toy remained top contender in its class. (Photo Courtesy Larry Schreib)

Grumpy's Toy XII made its debut in August at the *Popular Hot Rodding* Championship race held at Michigan. Running 8.80-second elapsed times, the Monza fell early in eliminations as Bill struggled to work out the new-car bugs.

Power for the new car continued to be provided by the 331-inch "little" block, featuring the now standard (but heavily modified) 660-cfm Holley carburetors mounted to an equally modified Edelbrock manifold. If you haven't figured it out by now, little of what went into building a *Grumpy's Toy* remained box stock; not engine components, Lenco transmissions, or the dipped-and-drilled Dana rear axle assembly. The cylinder heads resembled Chevrolet 292 castings and sported 2.05-inch-diameter intake valves supported by General Kinetics valve gear. Final compression was squeezed out to 14:1.

The match-race engine was now an iron-block 494-ci big-block. Bill had received a handful of these

John Jodauga flaunts his skills in this mid 1970s ad for Moroso products. By this point in Bill's career, it was hard to miss him in the monthly magazines. (Author Collection)

Grumpy's Toys 137

Chapter Five

4.4375-inch-bore blocks from Chevrolet in late 1971. They had been created as replacements for the aluminum 430-inch Can-Am block.

Roger Lamb redesigned the MacPherson strut suspension for the new Monza, lowering both the strut and lower control arm while simultaneously redesigning the arms. This allowed for additional exhaust header clearance along with a lower silhouette. Unlike the previous Vega, where notches were cut into the hood for strut clearance, the new Monza had all of its suspension components retained within the body.

Grumpy's Toy XII was the test car for one of the first Doug Nash clutchless 5-speed manual transmissions. Though initial tests showed it was easily .05 second quicker than the Lenco, reliability issues and later an NHRA ban ended this experiment. Jenkins stuck with the Lenco through his last *Toy* in 1983.

After a semifinals loss at the 1976 NHRA Winternationals, Jenkins finally relinquished the driver's seat to Larry Lombardo. At the time, the NHRA did not allow transfer of points gained from one driver to another. For the Jenkins/Lombardo duo, already one race into the season, it was a fresh start.

If nothing else, Jenkins had the suspension tuned in at Indy 1975. The Monza was eliminated early in competition due to new-car bugs. (Photo Courtesy Dave Milcarek)

Like the Vega before it, Grumpy's Monza used a well-balanced SRD chassis to produce record-setting 8-second quarter-mile times. The wind-cheating headlight covers were rejected by the NHRA, while the AHRA seemed to have no issue with Bill using them. To the rear of the car stands Jim Tice, late president of the AHRA. (Photo Courtesy John Eichinger)

The Pro Stocks: 1970–1983

John Jodauga served as Jenkins' public relations man throughout the 1970s. His artistic skills and vivid imagination showed up in some great press kits. Shown is the 1975 edition. (Bill Jenkins Collection)

Lombardo made his debut in grand fashion at the NHRA Gatornationals. He won the event and set a new national elapsed-time record in the process with an 8.71-second run.

Lombardo lowered the record again at the next two national events (the Summernationals and Grandnationals), first defeating the Vega of Andy Mannarino, and then the Hornet of Wally Booth with times of 8.68 and 8.59 seconds.

At NHRA's showcase event, the US Nationals, the Monza's hot streak came to an end after the 331-ci powerplant dropped a valve during eliminations.

At the season-ending 1976 World Finals, Team Jenkins saw their opportunity for the World Championship threatened by upstart Warren Johnson and his big-block–equipped Camaro. Johnson hadn't won a major event during the eight-race season but, due to points gained during the year, he was in the enviable position of being a possible upset victor if he could outlast Lombardo by three rounds.

Johnson met Lombardo in the first round of eliminations. Johnson held the number-2 qualifying position with an 8.82-second effort, and Lombardo had qualified the Monza in 10th position with an off-pace 8.93-second run. Lombardo's holeshot clipped Johnson's Camaro with a 9.00-second ET to a losing 8.91-second effort.

*Most of Grumpy's team pose with **Grumpy's Toy XII**. Left to right are mechanic Ron Thacker, driver Larry Lombardo, mechanic Rich Wright, machinist George Areford, and crew chief/foreman Joe Tryson. Missing from the picture is Ken Dondero, who was out on the road with Dave Christie and **Grumpy's Toy X**.* (Photo Courtesy Larry Schreib)

Chapter Five

Joe Tryson, who rarely took to the road, made the trip to Englishtown with Lombardo in 1977 for an early-season match race. Joe is seen here holding the Monza stationary while Larry warms the hides. (Photo Courtesy Steve Bell)

Ken Dondero dominated AHRA Pro Stock in 1975 and 1976 with **Grumpy's Toy X** and **Grumpy's Toy XII**. (Ken Dondero Collection)

Grumpy's Toy XII was raced through the 1976 season and is seen here at the NHRA Gatornationals. Larry Lombardo drove the Monza to the low qualifying position with an 8.73-second pass. (Photo Courtesy Thomas Nagy)

Grumpy's cars were always some of the nicest presented, and the latest **Toy** was no exception. Jack Trost applied the gorgeous pearl paint. (Photo Courtesy Tom Kasch)

At the 1976 Gatornationals, Warren "The Professor" Johnson made his first NHRA final-round appearance. Larry Lombardo played spoiler in Jenkins' Monza, defeating Johnson with a record-setting 8.71-second run to Warren's 8.76-second effort. (Photo Courtesy Dave Milcarek)

The Pro Stocks: 1970–1983

Grumpy's Toy XII was retired from NHRA competition after the 1976 season, and today resides at Don Garlits' Drag Racing Museum in Ocala, Florida. It remains in unrestored condition. (Photo Courtesy Rob Potter)

Grumpy's Toy XII was match raced into 1977. The car is sporting its second coat of paint, so the Grumpy's Toy signature is now located above the sponsor decals. (Photo Courtesy Tim McVay)

Grumpy's Toy XIII, 1976 Monza

America celebrated its bicentennial in 1976, and Jenkins also celebrated his team winning the AHRA and the NHRA Pro Stock Championships. There may have been a Ford in the White House, but, to fans of Chevrolet drag racing, there was a Chevy where it mattered.

Larry Lombardo took the NHRA Championship with *Grumpy's Toy XII*. Ken Dondero used *Grumpy's Toy XIII* for most of the season and, for the second year in a row, took the AHRA crown by winning 8 of the 10 national events. Just like in 1975, Dondero used *Grumpy's Toy XII* to close out the season.

In legal trim, Grumpy's Monzas all ran the same 331-inch-displacement engines, regardless of sanctioning body. For match race purposes, *Grumpy's Toy XIII* made due with a 354-ci small-block. The writing may have been on the wall for the small car/small-block combination though. The IHRA was the first sanctioning body to do away with weight breaks and go to an unlimited cubic-inch format.

In 1977, *Grumpy's Toy XIII* ran NHRA Pro Stock, starting the year off right with a Winternationals win and a new MPH record of 159.29.

Chapter Five

In July, during a match race at Oswega Dragstrip near Chicago, the Monza was severely damaged in a race-track incident.

Local racer Paul Dazzo was one of three randomly chosen contestants to run against Bill. Having grown up a fan of the Grump, this was a dream come true. Paul was running an LS7-powered 1969 Camaro and was realistic enough to know he didn't stand a chance against the Monza. When he asked Bill which lane he'd prefer, Bill stated that it didn't matter, he was going to beat him anyways. Ouch!

Larry Lombardo, making his way through the crowded pits of Maple Grove with Toy XIII. *He had a banner year, even capturing the NHRA Championship. The then-current weight breaks seemed as fair as they could be, making the Championship win that much sweeter.* (Photo Courtesy Bill Truby)

Inside the Oleynik hauler, showing some between-rounds thrashing during a 1977 match race. It truly was a "run what you brung" atmosphere—hoping you brought enough to come out on top. (Photo Courtesy Bill Truby)

The Pro Stocks: 1970–1983

Bill chose the right lane, and each car went through the pre-race ritual of heating the tires. Both cars staged and left the line together. It wasn't until third gear that Paul realized Bill wasn't beside him or in front of him, as he should have been. A look in the mirror showed Bill rolling off the track and into the guardrail. As recalled by the starter Bub Thurlby, it appeared that something in the Monza broke when Bill hit second gear. Bill recalled getting angry and instead of lifting (which, in hindsight, he should have), he kept his foot in it.

After being cut from the car, Bill was taken to a local hospital and treated for a couple of broken ribs and a few broken bones in his hand. The Monza was loaded up and shipped back to Malvern for repairs.

Luck went from bad to worse for *Grumpy's Toy XIII*. At the US Nationals in September, the Jenkins/Lombardo team had entered the race holding second place, behind Don Nicholson in the NHRA Pro Stock points standings. During a qualifying run, an inner tube in one of the slicks blew. This forced the Monza into the guardrail and it caught fire. There were no injuries, and thanks to the quick response of the track safety crew, the car was saved. However, it was in no condition to race. Fellow racer Ronnie Manchester, who had qualified a near-identical

Ron Thacker and Joe Tryson hold 'er steady while Bill heats the tires on **Grumpy's Toy XIII** *during a match race at Maple Grove in 1977.* (Photo Courtesy Bill Truby)

Though the outer damage was severe, the SRD-built chassis and roll cage held up and (for the most part) remained unscathed. (Photo Courtesy Bub Thurlby)

Oswega fans look on at the destruction. Bill had to be cut from the car, and couldn't walk away from this one. (Photo Courtesy Bub Thurlby)

Chapter Five

SRD-built Monza of his own, graciously loaned his car to Jenkins for eliminations. In a valiant effort to gain much-needed points on leader Don Nicholson, Lombardo re-qualified the Monza in the number-3 position, with an 8.71-second effort, using the transplanted drivetrain from *Grumpy's Toy*.

Nicholson and Lombardo met in the semifinals. If Lombardo could defeat Nicholson, he would have a shot at capturing the title. All efforts were to no avail though; Dyno Don's Mustang proved to be too much to overcome. Nicholson defeated Lombardo and went on to capture his one-and-only Pro Stock Championship. Lombardo finished the season in third position behind the other Ford guy, Bob Glidden.

Bill enjoyed his last national event win as a car owner in 1977, when Lombardo took the NHRA Summernationals by defeating the Monza of Frank Iaconio. Frank handed the win to Lombardo on the starting line, when he spun a tire off the axle.

Grumpy's Toy XIII *made an early exit from competition during the Springnationals in 1976.* (Photo Courtesy Tom Kasch)

Grumpy's Toy XIII *on the scales at Maple Grove in 1976.* (Photo Courtesy Bill Truby)

Wherever the Jenkins Competition crew went, a crowd followed. Here's a typical pit scene for Jenkins in 1976. He was credited as one of the first to erect barriers to keep the crowds at bay, allowing him and the crew room to work. Look at some of the older photos, and you can see why it was necessary. (Photo Courtesy Larry Schreib)

At the same race, *Grumpy's Toy XII* initially failed technical inspection due to the "funny" heads bolted onto his 331. Bill said, "We were in the middle of the Bowtie head development program, and I had some modified 292 heads on the car that they didn't like. I had previously gone up to Saginaw and took a bunch of 292 water jacket bores and filed away where we didn't want the water to be. This allowed for additional room to port." It was never satisfactorily explained why the heads were rejected, when you had Richard Maskin designing his own cylinder heads.

The Bowtie heads were developed in 1977 and 1978. Jenkins said that he received the first set of Bowtie heads, which were raw-casting prototypes. "We toyed with those heads, taking them down to 18 degrees [of valve angle] but never ran them competitively, as there proved to be no advantage to it. There was too much of a turn inside the head, so any gain you made in the cylinder, you lost in the port." Jenkins went on to that at this point in Bowtie cylinder head development, they had yet to get into raising the ports.

At the Winternationals in 1978, some fine driving by Lombardo went to waste after losing to Bob Glidden in the final round. Glidden, who had been picking up steam since his first national event win in 1973, rolled into Pomona and grabbed the low qualifying position with a 8.59-second effort. Lombardo,

Joe Tryson and Dave Christie make some between-round adjustments to the twin Holley carbs. Dave spent a year on the road traveling the AHRA circuit with Ken Dondero, while Joe rarely traveled far from home. (Author Collection)

Larry Lombardo battles it out with Bobby Yowell in Billy Stepp's Hemi-powered Plymouth Arrow. The NHRA finally allowed the short-wheelbase Chrysler import into the Pro Stock mix in 1977. It didn't help Chrysler's cause, but did add variety. (Author Collection)

Also at Maple Grove. The "Formula 5000"-style hood scoop ensured the match-race 494-ci stroker big-block received plenty of clean air. (Photo Courtesy Bill Truby)

Chapter Five

slightly off his usual pace, qualified the Team Jenkins Monza in 12th position with an 8.83-second elapsed time. Showcasing the skills that got him the driving job in the first place, Lombardo waded through a tough field of qualifiers to come face to face with Glidden and his now-dominant Fairmont. Both cars left the line nearly even, but Glidden's Cleveland Ford had just a little more top end and pulled away from Lombardo with a decisive 8.67-second run at 156.52 mph to an 8.78-second run at 155.70 mph.

Glidden marched on, going undefeated after his Springnationals loss to take his third Championship in four years. Jenkins summed up Glidden's winning ways by saying he just never quit. He was deserving of his wins because he worked at it 24/7.

There was no national event win to show for their efforts in 1978. But the Jenkins/Lombardo

Grumpy's Toy XIII *had fallen out of serious contention by the time the US Nationals rolled around in 1978, thanks to the less-than-favorable weight breaks given to the small-block-powered, short-wheelbase car. By this point in the year, Jenkins had his next creation on the building block.* (Photo Courtesy Bill Truby)

Grumpy's Toy *at Cayuga, Ontario, Canada, in 1977 for a WCS points meet. How many years has it been since crew members were allowed to be this close to a car during the burnout ritual?* (Photo Courtesy Rob Potter)

The Pro Stocks: 1970-1983

Grumpy's Toy XIII *runs against Don Nicholson's shotgun Mustang II. Nicholson's Mustang II was the first match racer to run 7s. The whereabouts of the Monza is unknown.* (Photo Courtesy Mike Sopko)

combo finished the year at number-2 in the Pro Stock standings, based on their four national event second-place finishes.

As reported *in Car Craft* magazine at the time, prior to the Summernationals, Pro Stock drivers held a meeting to discuss the future of the category. Bill suggested limiting carburetion to a single 4-barrel. Maybe he was disillusioned with the way the category was evolving, or changing as the stockers had into Factory Experimental and Funny Cars. His idea was squashed and at the conclusion of the meeting, indecisive minds prevailed and Pro Stock continued to evolve as it has.

What may be deemed as a little more far-fetched was Bill's idea to have the three professional categories divided and each run by a sanctioning body. An example would have been the AHRA running Funny Cars, IHRA running Pro Stocks, and the NHRA running Top Fuelers. How we would have gotten each sanctioning body to go along with this plan escapes me.

Grumpy's Toy XIV, 1977 Monza

Grumpy's latest (and last) Monza was built specifically to fulfill the demands of match racing. The engine had a 4 7/16-inch-bore, 494-ci big-block,

Another shot of the match-race-configured car at Englishtown, New Jersey, this time with Bill behind the wheel. Jenkins was a true innovator in the sport of drag racing, and was never afraid to think outside the box or look elsewhere for fresh ideas. (Photo Courtesy Steve Bell)

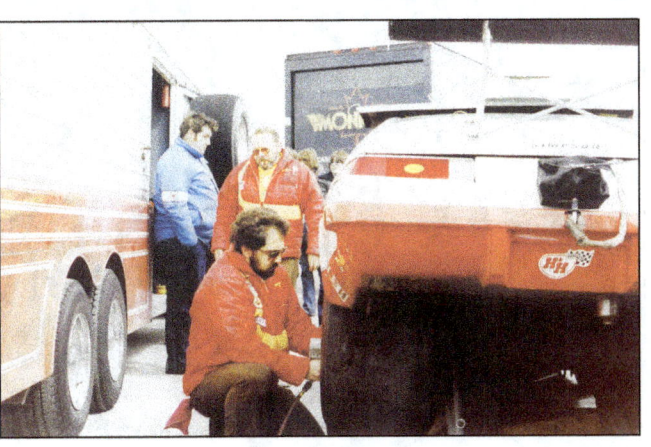

With its 19x32-inch tires and road race wing, the match race Monza was looking more like the Funny Cars that Bill had feared Pro Stock would morph into. (Photo Courtesy Rob Potter)

Grumpy's Toys 147

Chapter Five

and, by Bill's own estimate, was producing in the neighborhood of 900 hp. Generally, the match race engines were never bolted to the engine dyno, so their actual output cannot be confirmed. Backing up the big-inch engine was a Lenco 5-speed and a Ford 9-inch rear differential, usually carrying 5.57:1 gears.

Bill's involvement in match racing had started back in 1958 with a couple races each year. He credited Arnie "The Farmer" Beswick, who would run locals out at Lancaster and York, as being the original match racer.

By 1966, Jenkins was running six to eight matches per year, a number that built slowly until it peaked in the mid 1970s at 40 to 50 annually. Jenkins said that the number of match races only died off when the number of national events increased, and sponsors insisted they show for them.

Financially, due to guaranteed payouts, match racing proved to be far more lucrative than running national events. The match-race payouts ranged from $5,000 for a single race up to $12,000 for a three-day weekend. Bill said that they were match racing like crazy through this time. In 1976 alone, he had racked up 188 days in hotel rooms and close to 200,000 airline miles.

Bill, cruising through the pits on his trusted minibike. This scene was repeated throughout the 1970s. Reports of Bill and the bike making an occasional jaunt down hotel hallways have never been substantiated, or denied. (Photo Courtesy Rob Potter)

March 1978 was the first time out for the match race car. Seen here at Englishtown, Jenkins holds on while Lombardo warms the tires. (Photo Courtesy Steve Bell)

The Pro Stocks: 1970–1983

Grumpy's Toy XIV at Cayuga Raceway in Ontario, Canada. Note the For Sale sign on the quarter window, and the poorly fitting fiberglass panels. (Photo Courtesy Rob Potter)

Having dismissed Lombardo the previous season, Jenkins was back in the driver's seat in 1980. Bill is seen here lifting the wheels at the NHRA Gatornationals in 1980. (Photo Courtesy Steve Bell)

One of the few cars unaccounted for, the match-race Monza disappeared after Jenkins sold it in 1980. (Photo Courtesy Rob Potter)

"Winged Express" turned 7-second quarter-mile times before its retirement in 1980. (Photo Courtesy Dave Milcarek)

Chapter Five

To help get the Monza down to its minimum 1,900-pound weight, Bill and crew extensively used fiberglass paneling. The metal panels that did remain on the car were acid dipped in a tank built next door at SRD. As a personal first, Bill finally put fiberglass doors on the car. The poor-fitting doors were gutted and never equipped for windows or handles. At this same time, the car received a fiberglass 1978 Monza front clip.

Back behind the wheel for the 1980 NHRA Winternationals, Bill found that the "Lotus car" liked to stand up, losing valuable elapsed time in the process. (Photo Courtesy www.LesWelch.com)

*Jenkins rattles the eyeballs while heating the Firestones of his 494-powered match-race Camaro. Form did not always fit function, but you knew no matter how out of place it may have looked, if it was on **Grumpy's Toy**, it worked.* (Photo Courtesy Tim McVay)

Jenkins raced the Monza through 1980. He occasionally ran IHRA races, where he piloted the car to a quick 7.975-second best ET at 166.66 mph.

Grumpy's Toy XV, 1979 Camaro

Due to a revision of NHRA Pro Stock rules that favored the long-wheelbase and small-ci-motor combination, Jenkins said goodbye to the Monza and built a new Camaro for the 1979 season. This was the last year for the tried-and-true 331-ci small-block that was now producing 700 hp. The 331 propelled the latest *Toy* to times in the 8.60-second range. This was a long way from the 1972 Winternationals-winning engine that produced 540 hp and 9.40-second elapsed times.

Larry Lombardo enjoyed the nighttime air while qualifying Jenkins' Camaro at the NHRA Summernationals in 1979. (Photo Courtesy Steve Bell)

In his last major race behind the wheel, Larry Lombardo lost to Bob Glidden in the finals at the NHRA US Nationals in 1979. Referring to Larry, Bill noted, "Losing a race did not get him fired." (Photo Courtesy Tom Kasch)

This rare 1979 photo shows Dyno Don Nicholson and his Fox-bodied Mustang getting nipped by eventual runner-up Larry Lombardo. Dyno, the consummate sportsman, was described by Bill as someone you couldn't dislike. (Photo Courtesy Tom Kasch)

Chapter Five

Grumpy's Toy XV is seen here at the 1980 NHRA Summernationals, held at Raceway Park, New Jersey. An experiment in chassis design didn't turn out as well as Bill hoped. "For starters, a four-link probably would have been a better route to go." (Photo Courtesy Steve Bell)

Bill attempted to take advantage of the ever-changing NHRA weight breaks and built a small-inch-displacement Camaro. He made his annual pilgrimage west and introduced the Camaro at the season-opening NHRA Winternationals in 1979. (Photo Courtesy Rob Potter)

Bob Glidden traded in his Ford Fairmont for a Plymouth Arrow in 1979 and grabbed the NHRA Pro Stock Championship for the second year in a row. Bill noted that Bob was a fierce competitor, worked hard, and earned whatever he got. By the looks of this photo, he may have come out on the short end this time around. (Photo Courtesy Mike Sopko)

The Pro Stocks: 1970-1983

The mouse that roared was backed by the Lenco 5-speed transmission (now standard equipment) and a Ford 9-inch rear end, housing 5.57:1 gears. For match racing, Jenkins relied on the same 494-inch big-blocks that he had since 1971.

The 1979 Camaro was often referred to as "the Lotus car," due to its unique frame design. Like Lotus Engineering's race cars, the drivetrain was used as a main torsional support. Total weight of the bare frame was a light 135 pounds. Starting at the rear, Bill decided to forego his patented three-link suspension for a ladder-bar setup. The ladder-bar eyes bolted to a crossmember, which doubled as the rear transmission mount. This allowed the rear axle reaction torque to go up through the transmission and engine instead of through the frame back up to the engine. In hindsight, Bill feels the ladder-bar rear suspension was a mistake. "You had to stand the car up about 3 feet to make it run, and you'd be pulling second gear in midair."

The transmission had a large extension, which Bill had fabricated out of five hollowed Lenco cases. This moved weight to the rear of the car, and placed

Bill and his Grumpy's Toy cars would be regular visitors north of the border. Here, the Camaro's tires are warmed at Toronto Motorsport Park (Cayuga, Ontario) during a scheduled NHRA points meet. (Photo Courtesy Rob Potter)

Grumpy's Toy XV was sold at the end of 1980 and ended up with an Oldsmobile body over its tube chassis. Its whereabouts are unknown. (Photo Courtesy Tom Kasch)

Grumpy's Toys

Chapter Five

*Joe Lepone, Jr., took over the reins of **Grumpy's Toy** in 1982. By his own admission, after the first run he convinced himself he couldn't drive the car. Joe obviously caught on quickly, finishing in the top five at the majority of NHRA events attended.* (Author Collection)

Ray Allen departed on less-than-ideal terms in 1981, after a dismal year behind the wheel. (Photo Courtesy Bill Truby)

Grumpy's Toys

The Pro Stocks: 1970–1983

Bill's 572-inch Rodeck "mountain motor," which was used for match racing and was also legal for the IHRA Pro Stock class. Note the provision in the intake manifold for nitrous oxide connection. The nitrous was sprayed once during a match race and melted a number of pistons. (Photo Courtesy Steve Johns)

the transmission beside the driver. The idea had originated in 1975 when Bill toyed with the idea of running a rope drive back to a Doug Nash 5-speed transmission.

The first use of the new layout was attempted at the NHRA Winternationals, where it was soundly rejected by tech inspectors. To satisfy the NHRA, the transmission was bolted back onto the bellhousing, and a large tube, which bolted up to the rear crossmember, was placed behind the transmission. The NHRA revised its rules, due to Bill's "thinking outside of the box," in a move to prevent others from doing the same.

Larry Lombardo was runner-up at the NHRA Springnationals and the US Nationals in 1979, after which Jenkins dismissed Larry and took back the reins. Contrary to popular belief at the time, Larry was not dismissed because of the Indy loss. Rather, he was let go because of one too many disagreements

Bill, Steve Johns, and rookie driver Joe Lepone, Jr., traveled to the IHRA race in Rockingham in 1981. IHRA rules were a little more liberal than the other sanctioning bodies and allowed for unlimited cubic inches. (Photo Courtesy Steve Johns)

Chapter Five

with the boss. Or, as an ex-employee put it, "He forgot who the boss was." At the end of it all, Bill had nothing but praise for the driving skills of Lombardo. Larry went on to minor Pro Stock success of his own before retiring to the business of building oval-track racing engines.

The time away from the pilot's seat had a detrimental effect on Bill's driving skills. He could see how his reflexes had deteriorated and, with failing vision, he was guessing at the tree. Bill went nearly three years without success on the national level, as Pro Stock became very much a two-team show. Bob Glidden and the Reher/Morrison/Shepherd teams pretty much rolled over everyone else in the class. To stay competitive, Bill needed to find a new driver.

Ray Allen, who had recently driven his own Pro Stock car, was hired late in the season to fill the vacant seat. Ray had gained initial fame in the early 1970s by dominating Super Stock with his Truppi/Kling–prepared, 454-powered 1970 Chevelle. In 2006, this same Chevelle fetched $1.2 million at the Barrett-Jackson auto auction in Arizona.

The Camaro made a dismal showing, by Jenkins' standards. It finished the 1980 season holding 7th place in NHRA Pro Stock standings.

Grumpy's Toy XVI, 1981 Camaro

Famed chassis builder Don Ness was hired to bend the tubing into shape for the latest *Toy*, a car that Bill referred to as faultless. "No matter where we ran it, the car could be unloaded and taken down the track with very little having to be done." The car was introduced at the season opener at Englishtown, New Jersey. The Jenkins Super Crew bolted in the

Bill switches up the slicks while Joe prepares for yet another run. With a new driver in place for the 1982 season, Bill hoped to reestablish himself as a serious threat. His creditability suffered after slipping to seventh in the NHRA Pro Stock standings the previous season. (Photo Courtesy Francis Butler)

Steve Johns and Joe Lepone, Jr., plug away on the 500-inch creation that powered Grumpy's Toy in 1982 and 1983. Fuel delivery would be handled by a pair of Holley dominators feeding through a Holley intake manifold. (Photo Courtesy Francis Butler)

match race Rodeck and banged off 7.80-second elapsed times.

The car, in legal NHRA trim, was powered by a 4.25-inch-bore, destroked big-block displacing 363 inches. It was backed up by the Lenco 5-speed and a Ford 9-inch rear end. Taking advantage of the revised NHRA cubic-inch rules for the 1982 season, the Camaro ran anywhere from 494 to the maximum 500 ci, and produced approximately 1,000 hp. The Camaro was raced into early 1983, with Joe Lepone, Jr., taking over the driving chores at the beginning of the 1982 season.

For match racing and IHRA Pro Stock use, Jenkins built a 572-ci aftermarket Rodeck block featuring a 4.50-inch bore and stroke. In 1981, Ray Allen drove the Camaro to an IHRA-legal best time of 7.899 seconds at 176.82 mph.

The 1981 season was forgettable for the Grump. The team finished seventh in the NHRA Pro Stock standings, with four DNQs out of the seven national events the team entered. It was one of Jenkins' worst seasons on record. Sponsors, previously easy to find, also recognized this and began jumping ship. Bill attempted to right the situation in 1982 by putting a new driver behind the wheel.

Joe Lepone, Jr., was introduced to Bill in 1981 through Ray Allen. Joe, who had been running a D/Gas Vega and had befriended Ray at the racetrack, bumped into him one evening and was invited to drop by Jenkins' shop to check out the latest *Toy*. He came over around 11 pm one evening, Ray introduced Joe to Bill, and pleasantries were exchanged. A couple weeks later, Joe was back at Jenkins Competition for his first introduction to the real Grump. Joe recalled, "Coming in the side door, I spot Bill, who is at a work bench looking over a cylinder head. I say, 'Hi, Bill, how are you doin'?' He lets out an 'mmmph.' I stop, turn around, and say, 'Yo, Bill, mmmph to you too; I guess that means hello around here.' That was my official introduction to the Grumpy one, and from that point forward we got along great."

Joe tagged along with the team, helping out at the track and impressing Jenkins along the way with his "get it done" work ethic. But 10 days prior to the NHRA US Nationals, Ray Allen decided to take some time off to help his former partner Frank Iaconio build an engine for his own Pro Stock Camaro. Frank went on to qualify the car at Indy with an 8.53-second pass while Ray, in *Grumpy's Toy*, could do no better than an 8.75. This placed *Grumpy's Toy* in the 16th

The Don Ness–built **Grumpy's Toy XVI** *made an appearance at Indy in 1982, where Joe Lepone, Jr., was eliminated in the quarter finals.* (Photo Courtesy Steve Johns)

Chapter Five

and final qualifying position. Ray red lighted all hopes away in the first round of eliminations. It was the beginning of the end of his relationship with Jenkins. After another lackluster performance at the NHRA Golden Gate Nationals, Joe was asked to take over behind the wheel for the 1982 season. Reluctant at first, Joe finally agreed. Ray Allen's final ride in *Grumpy's Toy* proved to be the NHRA World Finals, where the car failed to qualify.

Joe Lepone, Jr., had no real interest in driving a Pro Stocker. Instead, he saw his future behind the wheel of a Funny Car. He was friends with late Funny Car owner/driver "Jungle" Jim Liberman, and had spent a lot of time at Jungle's shop behind the wheel of his flip-top Monza, dreaming of the day. Prior to actually driving *Grumpy's Toy*, Joe had to earn his professional license, so plans were made to head over to Englishtown, New Jersey, late in October to get it done.

Having never operated a Lenco transmission before, Joe followed Bill's lead in regard to how the car should be shifted. The instructions were to pull the first lever, then push the second, and finally pull the third. So each night for a week prior to Englishtown, Joe headed down to Jenkins' shop after everyone had gone home and practiced. "I would take the carburetor linkage off and install a spring on the gas pedal, put on my fire suit and helmet, and buckle myself into the car, just like I was heading out to race." With the car on the hoist 3 to 4 feet off the ground, Joe added his own sound effects as he practiced away on the Lenco. The fourth night into it, he was banging off the gears and finishing off another imaginary run to the sound of his own

It's 1983, and 500-inch Pro Stockers were the rule of the day. Lepone, in his second year of driving a Pro car, helped ensure that Jenkins finished out his career as a car owner in the top five. (Bill Jenkins Collection)

The Pro Stocks: 1970–1983

wailing voice when he heard a voice behind him, "Was that a good one?" Bill was standing behind him, watching in full amusement.

On the last weekend in October, Joe, Bill, and Joe Tryson headed to Englishtown to get a license for Joe. Prior to doing so, Bill had them pull the "good" 363 engine out of the car and install the number-3 engine. The number-3 engine was considered to be the slowest. With the engine swapped and an old set of Firestones installed, off they went.

The quickest NHRA-legal time the Camaro had run that year was at the Indy Nationals, where Ray Allen had turned an 8.75-second pass in a losing cause. For Joe, who had never driven the car at all (excluding his imaginary runs), the pressure was on. Joe recalled, "I had come out of a Vega race car with a full interior. This Camaro, with all its tin work, was a rattle trap, shaking and vibrating like you wouldn't believe. I get out of the car after driving up the staging lanes and tell Joe [Tryson], I don't want to drive this thing."

Tryson, like a mother sending her child off to school alone for the first time, convinced Lepone, Jr., that all would be fine.

Joe heated up the Firestone slicks for the customary burnout, staged the car, and followed Jenkins' suggestion by leaving the line at 8,500 rpm. He recalled, "Somehow I survive the run and make it back to the pits and there is Bill standing there with his arms crossed. I get out of the car and tell him, 'I can't drive this thing; I don't want to drive this thing.' And he starts laughing. Bill says, 'What do you mean?' So I tell him, 'I put this thing in third and the car wants to go everywhere. I did the stupidest thing ever.' Bill says, 'What's that?' I say, 'I put it in high gear.' This is when he tells me I went an 8.66. I responded that I don't care if I went 8.26, I don't want to drive this thing."

Bill told Joe that he didn't think he was going to make a full pass. Joe, who didn't understand what that had to do with anything, listened as Bill told him that the Firestone slicks he put on the car were last run in 1978. A tire change was made and, after some sweet talk, Joe was convinced to make another run.

Joe came off the line at 8,500 rpm, shifted at 8,900, and his second run netted an incident-free 8.60-second timeslip. The third run, with 180 degrees of water temperature and 70 psi of oil pressure, delivered an 8.57-second elapsed time. This was almost two tenths of a second quicker than the car had run all year, and only four hundredths of a

Joe Lepone, Jr., wheels the final Toy **at the** Popular Hot Rodding *magazine meet in the summer of 1983. The lack of key sponsors had carried over from the previous ride. This eased Bill's decision to sell the car.* (Photo Courtesy Mike Sopko)

Chapter Five

second off the national record. By the end of the day, Joe had produced a pair of 8.54-second timeslips and earned his competition license.

Jenkins Competition stayed away from the 1982 NHRA Winternationals, choosing instead to introduce the new driver in February during a match against Ronnie Sox in Baton Rouge, Louisiana. Ronnie and his Boss-powered Mustang had been cleaning Jenkins' clock, turning times in the 7.80-second range while Jenkins/Allen (who were running a 500-inch Bowtie aluminum big-block) had run no better than 8.16-second times.

Excluding the last half-dozen miles of the trip to Baton Rouge, Joe, who was traveling alone with Bill, drove the full 28 hours. It never failed that, within a few miles from the track gate, they had to find a convenience store so Bill could pick up cigars. From that point on, Jenkins drove the truck, making a grand entrance for his adoring fans at the track—a cigar in his mouth, and his arm out the window. The fans sucked this stuff up. Bill shamelessly admitted it was all an ego thing back then.

At the track, Ronnie Sox approached Lepone, Jr., congratulating him on the new job driving for Jenkins and asking whether he wanted to stage first or last. Joe, playing it cocky as only a new guy would, said to Ronnie, "You're not going to ask me that next month in Rockingham, so why are you asking me that now?" Joe wished Ronnie a safe ride and hopped back in *Grumpy's Toy*, all to Bill's amusement.

Satisfied with the pre-stage burnouts, Ronnie staged first, confident in his abilities to put the new kid in his place. The lights came down and off they went. To Ronnie's shock, Lepone beat him with a 7.77-second pass at 177.77 mph. At the time, this was the quickest ET ever turned by a Pro Stocker.

Ronnie swore the Camaro was running nitrous oxide. But back in the pits, Jenkins removed the hood for Ronnie so he could prove himself wrong. Joe made it two in a row, backing up the first win with a 7.78-second run.

Back in the pits, Bill commented to Joe on the need to sell more T-shirts, saying, "You don't mind being up in the air do you? Because I'm going to loosen the front end and adjust the wheelie bars."

So Joe did his burnout, staged, waited for the green light, and away he went. The Camaro pulled the front wheels 5 feet in the air, and then

The last known whereabouts of the Camaro was in the San Diego area, where Bob Panella had sold the car. (Rob Potter Photo)

The Pro Stocks: 1970–1983

slammed back down, taking out the oil pan. The damage was repaired with the help of racers' tape, silicone, and rags. How did Bill react? Well, he did sell a lot more T-shirts.

Joe ended the day with a clean sweep over Sox, producing a 7.75-second ET on the final run. The following week in Houston, the pair raced again with similar results, Joe taking Ronnie in a best two out of three. In match race trim, Joe won close to 90 percent of his races in 1982, re-establishing Jenkins Competition as a force to be reckoned with.

Though no NHRA national events were won in 1982, *Grumpy's Toy XVI* usually made the top five and finished out the season holding fifth position in the points standings. This was due in part to semifinal finishes at both the Summernationals and World Finals. The Camaro was sold to Joe Clark early in 1983, and has since disappeared from the scene.

Grumpy's Toy XVII, 1983 Camaro

The final *Grumpy's Toy* was built by Joe and Marty Signorelli of Diamond Race Cars in Long Island, New York. The drivetrain in the Camaro remained basically unchanged from 1982, with 500 inches of NHRA-legal big-block providing the go. As usual, Jenkins' engines used only the best parts, including a pair of Holley 1,050-cfm Dominator carburetors mounted on a heavily modified Holley intake manifold. A Competition Cams roller camshaft actuated the Manley valves, while Venolia pistons squeezed out 14:1 compression. A Lenco transmission, backed by a Ford 9-inch rear end carrying 5.17:1 (or greater) gears completed the drivetrain. The Jenkins three-link rear suspension was long gone, replaced by a four-link setup. A 4.4375-inch bore, 634-ci sleeved, Rodeck tall-deck engine was built for match race and IHRA competition. Jenkins recalls using John Deere wet sleeves, originally made for 4.25-bore diesel engines, in this block. "John Deere had a reputation for doing very good work, and the sleeves, which cost next to nothing, were available at any John Deere dealership."

Lepone ran a quick 7.66-second run at 180.72 mph with the car, and saw his greatest success come at the NHRA Southern Nationals. There, he played runner-up to Lee Shepherd in the Reher & Morrison Camaro. In Bill's opinion, this was a good time for

Bill gets comfortable behind the wheel as he discusses the ins and outs of campaigning a Pro Stocker with new owner Bob Panella. Jenkins' involvement with the Panella/Dondero team waned as corporate involvement increased. (Photo Courtesy Steve Johns)

Chapter Five

Pro Stock because the new rules had made it the closest and tightest form of racing there was. "You get the 16 quickest cars running each other within 6 or 7 hundredths of a second and it made for a very good show." With Joe Lepone, Jr., pulling the levers on the Lenco, Jenkins Competition again finished the NHRA season holding on to fifth place.

Joe called it quits at the season's end. He had been fighting the urge to strike out on his own for some time. Jenkins also decided he'd had enough. He was tired, and felt his heart was no longer into maintaining a car, let alone going through the motions of hiring yet another driver.

The "For Sale" sign went up on *Grumpy's Toy XVII* prior to the NHRA World Finals in Pomona, California, the car's final race in the hands of Jenkins. California resident Bob Panella, who was looking to go Pro Stock racing, bought it in conjunction with Ken Dondero. The pair's ties dated back more than two decades; Ken had driven Panella's BB/GS Anglia to the 1969 NHRA Winternationals Super Eliminator win.

Though Ken had been running a successful tire business for the previous eight years, he was entertaining an offer to sell; the stress of the business was killing him. He was aware *Grumpy's Toy XVII* was for sale, and after some back-and-forth discussion, the pair headed east to Jenkins Competition. A deal was struck to buy the car lock, stock, and barrel. Ken said, "We probably bought 75 percent of the stuff Bill had at the time. Everything but the trailer, as Bob had his own."

The car was housed at Jenkins Competition, with Bill doing the maintenance on the engines. Ken Dondero rented an apartment in town and came into the shop to do whatever work on the car that needed to be done. Initially, Bill assisted with tuning the car at national events. But due to conflicts with his ongoing work with Chevrolet on the V-6 program, this didn't last for long.

Panella had little success with the car, and eventually sold the body-and-chassis combo. He later installed the Jenkins engines in a Firebird leased from Ronnie Manchester.

Joe Lepone, Jr., and Bill pose with the final **Grumpy's Toy** *and* **Old Reliable IV**. *Bill missed the market and sold* **Old Reliable** *just before the prices started to escalate for such cars.* (Photo Courtesy Francis Butler)

Jeff Hensley's Busch Grand National Monte Carlo, driven by Mike Swaim. Mike, with Jenkins power, grabbed the pole position at the 1988 Busch Grand National Goodys 300 race held at Daytona. (Photo Courtesy Steve Johns)

Chapter Six

Beyond the Toys

Bill continued his work with Chevrolet on V-6 engine development, which was a program that had started in 1980. Bill jumped into off-road parts development for the 60-degree version of the V-6, an engine he would go on to describe as a pain. "The program really didn't develop into much, as the engine was never designed to be anything more than a passenger car engine."

In addition to the 60-degree V-6 development, Bill also worked on the 90-degree engine, which showed initial success with Gene Felton in the Kelly American Series. This led him down a couple different paths, including work in the Busch Grand National series, where he prepared cars for the likes of Ken Schrader and Chuck Bown. Bown's Hensley Racing Grand Prix captured NASCAR's Busch Grand National Championship in 1990.

The 90-degree engine wasn't without fault either; there were initial problems relating to the crankshaft counterweights and the oiling system.

Jenkins said that they had issues with the engine kicking out main bearings and rod bearings. The front rod bearing was the worst in those engines until Jenkins discovered there was inadequate oil pressure at that point. More design changes resulted from the developmental work done by Jenkins.

Regarding the main bearing issue, Jenkins determined that, for an odd-fire engine, the counterweights were nowhere near where they needed to be, and orbital loading was chewing the bearings out at high engine speed. Part of Bill's own philosophy regarding main bearings, orbital loading, and counterweights in American V-series engines is that the crankshaft is way off in design. "We got back into the Pro Stock stuff around 2003 with eight counterweights. We shifted some of the weights off the end of the crank and moved them toward the center, which really helped."

The V-6 development program also led Bill into the NHRA Competition Eliminator class, where he saw more than his fair share of wins, building engines for the likes of Garley Daniels. In 1987, Daniels grabbed the NHRA Comp Eliminator Championship.

Bob Kaiser was another prominent competitor who chose to run a Jenkins Competition–built bent six. In 1989, Bob dominated the same category with his Chevy Camaro and won the Championship. He

A Jenkins-built 274-inch V-6 with 23-degree-valve-angle heads, raised ports, and a single 4-barrel carb on a highly modified cross-ram-type manifold. (Photo Courtesy Steve Johns)

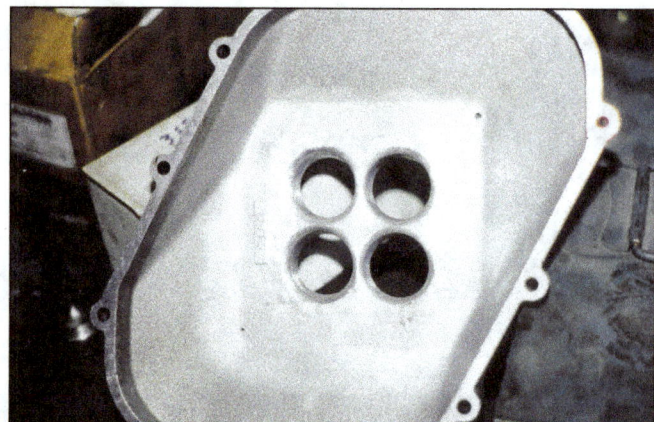
In 1988, NASCAR mandated restrictor plates and Jenkins went straight to the flow bench. What was once an open top had a matching four-hole design welded in. This design was probably worth 20 additional peak horsepower. (Photo Courtesy Steve Johns)

Chevrolet helped with this 1,700-pound, Jenkins Competition V-6–powered car to showcase its line of V-6 parts. This composite-bodied 1985 Camaro took Bob Kaiser to the NHRA Championship in 1989. (Photo Courtesy Steve Johns)

Beyond the Toys

Joe Tryson and Bill look on as Joe Lepone, Jr., powers his Camaro to its one and only NHRA national event win in 1985. (Photo Courtesy Steve Johns)

An 8-barrel setup for a V-6? Jenkins toyed with the idea in the mid 1980s, but it never got off the ground, or, in this case, the workbench. (Bill Jenkins Collection)

Another view of the same carburetor, which flowed 1,275 cfm. Where is this carb today? (Bill Jenkins Collection)

Chapter Six

repeated in 1992 with a D/Econo Dragster driven by Jenkins' employee, Steve Johns. It was an exciting time for Jenkins. He described it as a lot of fun because, "You're involved with every aspect of what's happening. Whatever part there is in that engine, it's a 'no excuse' part, and you're involved from the design stages through to completion."

An outcome of the Comp V-6 development was the carburetor vibration dampener. In lay terms, it was a piece of rubber placed between the carburetor and the manifold to isolate the carburetor (and thus the fuel) from the vibrations of the engine. The idea grew out of a curiosity about what or how fuel was reacting in the bowl. Jenkins was getting some weird numbers on the dyno, so he took a glass beaker and taped it onto the side of the carburetor. The vibrations broke the beaker.

Bill recalled, "Steve Johns played with it some, cutting rubber out and adding more fuel, which seemed to calm down the fuel curve and choke curve. The dampener was just one of those things that were proven, and you knew it should sell, but nobody would buy it. We tried to market it through Moroso for a few years, but the market just wasn't there. Now, I wouldn't even think about running a fabricated manifold without one."

Jenkins didn't completely ignore the Pro Stock class. He continued to build 500-inch engines through the late 1980s and saw the likes of Joe Lepone, Jr., and Gordie Riveria competing strongly with them. Success came as early as the NHRA World Finals in 1985, when Joe Lepone, Jr., won his first national-level event.

Bill readily admits his greatest satisfaction has come from his work with General Motors. With it, he says, unlike drag racing, you're not dealing with one or two units; you're dealing with issues that affect millions.

Jenkins saw his share of what he called "company cars" roll through the doors, starting with V-6–powered S-10 pickup trucks in the 1980s to the Corvettes in the 1990s. In 1988, General Motors was tooling up for the release of the new-generation V-8 engine due in 1990. Through Jenkins' input, Chevrolet made some fairly substantial and cost-effective changes. Jenkins suggested they add an oil gallery to the block—the current design was a mess. Bill described it as "a disaster waiting to happen."

Jenkins said there really wasn't anything new about the design change. It had originated with Chevrolet back in 1958 with the 348-ci engine. "They needed to put the gallery back up under the bottom of the water jacket. I brought the old microfiche files that I had received from engineering back in 1970 and suggested they do it the same way they had on the old aluminum-case 427. The change would take one compound angle out of the oil feed hole for the main bearings, and would save a bunch of money on tooling costs because it was a station stop on the transfer line just to put those holes in."

A Chevrolet tool supplier from Krupp asked Bill afterward, "Where did they find you?" Jenkins

A pair of 2-inch Dominator carburetors, modified by Jenkins. They feature 0.125-inch-overbored main bodies, throttles made in-house, re-contoured venturis, and narrowed throttle shafts. This was all accomplished in 1986, long before such carbs could be purchased, for use on Bill's 500-inch Pro Stock engines. (Photo Courtesy Steve Johns)

Here are some of the fruits of Bill's life's work. Taken in the late 1990s, this photo shows a few of Bill's personal toys, including a Model A Ford, an L-79–equipped Chevy II, and an LT-1–powered Corvette. (Bill Jenkins Collection)

quipped, "Oh, I just hang around here and make things happen."

Additional short-run projects were carried out through the mid 1990s, including work on the Generation II engine. Bill said, "We weren't doing any development work at that point; it was me machining up some parts so they could make the engines live. The pre-production blocks moved like crazy because there was no cylinder wall."

In 1995, Chevrolet was ramping up for production of the Corvette-only LT4 V-8 and had issues with blowby caused by poor ring seal. Jenkins built a few engines (for evaluation) that incorporated his volume-increasing groove. Chevrolet solved the initial blowby issue with a pre-production change in ring design, which, through evaluation, Bill had suggested. It sounds simple now, but Jenkins had them change the chamfer and the amount of twist the ring had. Jenkins' involvement in the Generation III small-block development was halted in favor of ramping up the Pro Stock Truck program.

Following the lead of NASCAR once again, the NHRA introduced its own Pro Stock Truck program in 1998, a program that Jenkins couldn't ignore. With his Comp Eliminator experience, he knew he could walk into the program and own it, and that's what he did. Between 1998 and 2001, Jenkins built a total of 33 358-ci lease engines for the likes of Larry Kopp, Mark Osborne, and Tim Freeman. Each of them won at least one national event.

The first time out for veteran Larry Kopp in his Jenkins-powered S-10 was the Fram Route 66 Springnationals at Dallas, Texas, where he took the win and set the MPH record at the same time. That season, Kopp won the Championship while recording times in the 7.60-second range. At one race, Larry was the number-1 qualifier, held low elapsed time and top speed of the race, set the ET and MPH records, and won the race. It was referred to as "a

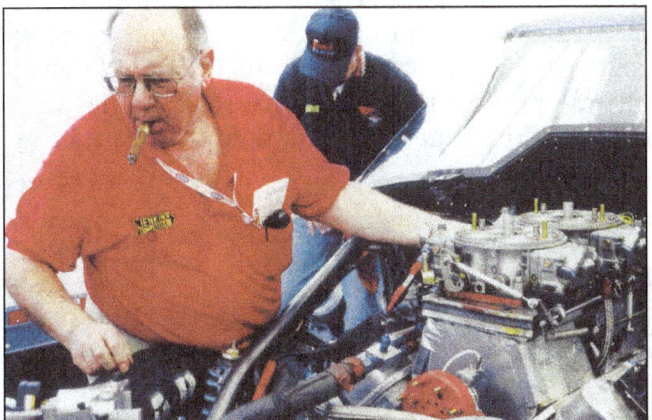
Victor Cagnazzi's Pro Stock Truck was powered by a Jenkins Competition 358-inch small-block. Seen here at Pomona in 2001, Bill followed through on a number of projects with Victor. (Photo Courtesy Steve Johns)

Vinny Barone took his Jenkins Competition–powered, Steve Johns–tuned S-10 to runner-up at the NHRA O'Reilly Fallnationals in 1999. (Photo Courtesy Thomas Nagy)

Chapter Six

full boat." It was a good day at the track; that's for sure.

With a bore of 4.1875 inches and stroke of 3¼ inches, Jenkins' truck engines were pulling 975 hp on the dyno by the time the program ended. The NHRA, not seeing the payoff they'd hoped for, pulled the plug on the Pro Stock Truck program in 2001. It was a hard pill for Jenkins to swallow. For him, it was $100,000 per month in business down the drain.

With a push from Steve Johns, Jenkins Competition got back into the thick of big-inch Pro Stock competition. Between May 2002 and November 2003, Bill developed a Pro Stock program in conjunction with Victor Cagnazzi. A couple of million dollars later, they were ready to race. Whoever said going Pro Stock racing was cheap?

Jim Yates, Dave Northrop, and Dave Connolly were beneficiaries of Jenkins' 500-inch engines, which were now producing a bit over 1,400 hp. Connolly qualified the first time out in May 2004, and went on to win three national events in his *Grumpy's Toy*–themed Cavalier. In 2005, Dave challenged for the NHRA Pro Stock crown, briefly holding the points lead and winning another three national events.

In 2008, with the nation's economy going south, Bill refocused his efforts and said goodbye to the Pro Stock engine program. For the foreseeable future, he plans to make small-block, V-6, and four-cylinder engine development his bread and butter. Bill's plans include putting the majority of his engines into Competition Eliminator cars unless, of course, he changes his mind.

While Bill looked on, Dave Northrop qualified his GTO at the 2008 NHRA TOYO Nationals, turning a 6.74-second elapsed time at 205 mph. (Photo Courtesy Michael "Mashie" Mihalko)

Is this the ultimate form of flattery? Dave Connolly painted his Jenkins-powered, national-event-winning Cavalier in the old **Grumpy's Toy** *paint scheme.* (Photo Courtesy Mike Sopko)

Over the years, the dyno at Jenkins Competition was well used. Extensive research and development was performed on everything from boat motors to 600-plus-ci Pro Stock engines. (Author Collection)

Epilogue

Though 153 Pennsylvania Avenue may no longer be the hotbed of activity it once was, the doors still swing open and the phone still rings after nearly 60 years of serving people seeking Bill's expertise.

Bill is grounded enough to know how fortunate he has been over the years. Sometimes though, like the rest of us, he thinks about what might have been if he had chosen a different path in life. But drag racing has never been something he ever seriously considered walking away from. He is rightfully proud of his accomplishments and retains a copy of every article ever written about him or the cars.

He's been quoted as saying, "I've never really done much in my life that I didn't want to do," and this holds true today. He goes to work five days a week because he wants to and, more often than not, he is the last one out the door at the end of the day. As this is written, Bill is approaching 80 years of age and shows no signs of letting up. Is he planning retirement? Not likely. "At this age, if I'm not doing this, I'm probably dead."

Numerous pet projects keep him busy—the dozen or so Quadrajet carburetors he has collected over the years, or the stealth *Grumpy's Toy XVIII* wagon out back. Carburetors have always been Bill's specialty, and he has the ability to leave a person dumbfounded as he rattles off part numbers, where the parts are used, and the interchangeability of each part. "The Quadrajet is a good carb; people just don't understand it and I think are afraid of it. We have done some in-house side-by-side comparisons and, on a good street engine, the Quadrajet will pull the Holley."

Bill has owned a station wagon every year since 1963, and the current one has been an ongoing plaything—carburetors or complete engines. To protect his daily-driven GTO from the harsh East Coast elements, the wagon is called into winter-time duty.

The past and present employees I talked to agreed that Bill is a good reader of people, and he can pick up on the ones worth investing in. More than one person said, if Bill saw the potential in you, he would invest in you and allow you the freedom to do more and learn more.

Bill has married twice and has three children. He likes to spend time away from the shop with family and friends. Still Grumpy after all these years? Yes and no. But as the sun sets on my recent visit to Jenkins Competition, I walk away feeling good—I have seen through the gruff facade. I was one of the lucky fans who had the opportunity to briefly visit his other side. Thanks for letting me in, Bill.

The nondescript Jenkins Competition facility as it looks today. If only the walls could talk!

Appendix

Grumpy's Toy Event Wins and Runners-Up

1965: NHRA Top Stock Winternationals win. Richmond Raceway S/S Championship (2,800-pound class). *Super Stock* Magazine Nationals (3,200-pound class) win.

1966: NHRA Winternationals runner-up. Springnationals runner-up. Indy Nationals runner-up. Super Stock Nationals win.

1967: AHRA Winternationals Middle Stock win (Chevy II). Super Stock Nationals win. NHRA Indy Nationals S/S win.

1968: NHRA World Finals runner-up in S/S (Bill driving the SS/D Nova). Street Eliminator runner-up (Ed Hedrick driving *Grumpy's Toy III* in modified production). Cecil County S/S Showdown win (*Grumpy's Toy III* with 427). *Cars* magazine runner-up.

1969: AHRA Springnationals win. Super Stock Nationals Experimental Super Stock win (*Grumpy's Toy IV*).

1970: NHRA Pro Stock Winternationals win. Gatornationals win. OCIR USA Pro Stock Championship win (all with *Grumpy's Toy IV*).

1971: Super Stock Nationals runner-up.

1972: NHRA Winternationals win. Springnationals win. Summernationals win. Grandnationals win. World Finals win. Supernationals win. NHRA Pro Stock World Champion. AHRA/PRA National Challenge win. IHRA Empire State Nationals win. IHRA Springnationals win. Super Stock Nationals win. *Cars* Magazine Championship.

1973: NHRA Summernationals win. World Finals runner-up. AHRA PRO National Challenge win.

1974: NHRA Winternationals (*Grumpy's Toy X*) win. Summernationals win. AHRA PRO National Challenge win. AHRA Winternationals runner-up.

1975: NHRA Springnationals win. Summernationals win. World Finals runner-up. AHRA Grand American West win. American Challenge win. Grand Nationals win. Summer Nationals win. World Finals win. Gateway Nationals runner-up. AHRA Pro Stock World Championship win (Ken Dondero driving).

1976: NHRA Gatornationals win. Summernationals win. Grand Nationals win. NHRA Pro Stock World Champion (Larry Lombardo driving). AHRA Show Me Nationals win. Springnationals win. Gateway Nationals win. AHRA Nationals at Green Valley win. World Finals win. Winternationals, Okie Nationals runner-up. AHRA Pro Stock World Championship (Ken Dondero driving). Professional Drivers Organization Race win (Ken Dondero driving).

1977: NHRA Winternationals win. Summernationals win, Gatornationals runner-up. Grand Nationals runner-up. AHRA Gateway Nationals win.

1978: NHRA Winternational runner-up. Summernationals runner-up. Grand Nationals runner-up. World Finals runner-up. PHR Championship runner-up.

1979: NHRA Springnationals runner-up. US Nationals runner-up.

1983: NHRA Southern Nationals runner-up.

NHRA Divisional Races Won by Bill Jenkins

1967: NHRA Super Stock—Englishtown, New Jersey; Sanford, Maine.

In 1971, it was not a good year to be running a Pro Stock Chevy, or Ford for that matter. The Chevrolet faithful never lost hope in the Grump, however. (Photo Courtesy Bill Truby)

Appendix

1968: NHRA Street Eliminator—Capitol Raceway; York, Pennsylvania; Connecticut Dragway.
1969: NHRA Super Stock—Maple Grove; Island Raceway.
1972: NHRA Pro Stock—ATCO.
1973: NHRA Pro Stock—ATCO.
1980: NHRA Pro Stock—MIR.

Winners Prepared by Jenkins Competition

1962: Dave Strickler—SS/S NHRA Nationals.
1963: Dave Strickler—A/FX NHRA Nationals, Little Eliminator NHRA Nationals, A/S NHRA Winternationals (O.R. 2).
1964: Dave Strickler—A/FX NHRA Nationals, AHRA Summernationals S/S Optional, Winternationals.
1967: George Cureton—NHRA Stock World Finals, Stock World Champion.
1968: Dave Strickler—NHRA Super Stock World Finals, Super Stock World Champion.
1969: Bill Morgan–Stock Eliminator NHRA US Nationals. Gary Kimball—AHRA Super Stock (heads-up) Nationals win, AHRA World Finals win, AHRA Championship (ex-*Grumpy's Toy III*-Jenkins ZL-1).
1970: Ed Hedrick—Super Stock NHRA Gatornationals, Jay Wheatley AHRA GT-1 Winternationals.
1985: Joe Lepone, Jr.—Pro Stock NHRA World Finals.
1987: Garley—Daniels Competition Eliminator NHRA Keystone Nationals, US Nationals, Comp Eliminator World Champion.
1988: Bob Kaiser—Comp Eliminator NHRA Summernationals.
1989: Bob Kaiser—Comp Eliminator NHRA Keystone Nationals, NHRA Winston Invitational, NHRA Comp Eliminator World Champion.
1991: Garley Daniels—Comp Eliminator NHRA Winston Invitational.
1992: Bob Kaiser—Competition Eliminator NHRA Springnationals, Grand Nationals. Steve Johns—Competition Eliminator NHRA Summernationals, NHRA Winston Invitational, NHRA Comp Eliminator World Champion.
1993: Charlie Greco—Comp Eliminator NHRA Keystone Nationals.
1995: Mark Osborne—Pro Stock NHRA Fram Nationals.
1997: Kevin Robb—Comp Eliminator NHRA Keystone Nationals. Charlie Greco—Comp Eliminator NHRA Mopar Parts Nationals.
1998: Larry Kopp—Pro Stock Truck NHRA Fram Route 66 Nationals, Mopar Parts Nationals, Revell Nationals, US Nationals, NHRA Pro Stock Truck World Champion. Brad Jeter—Pro Stock Truck NHRA Winston Finals. Tim Freeman—NHRA Pro Stock Truck Sears Craftsman Nationals.
1999: Steve Johns—Pro Stock Truck NHRA Auto Club Finals. Brad Jeter—Pro Stock Truck NHRA Fall Nationals, Auto Zone Nationals, Pennzoil Nationals. Brian Browell—Comp Eliminator NHRA Souther Nationals. Mark Osborne—Pro Stock Truck NHRA Gatornationals, O'Reilly Nationals.
2000: Steve Johns—Pro Stock Truck NHRA O'Reilly Fallnationals. Dave Northrop—Comp Eliminator NHRA Matco Tools Springnationals, Supernationals. Brian Browell—Comp Eliminator NHRA Southern Nationals. Jeff Sexton—Super Stock NHRA Route 66 Nationals.
2001: Brian Browell—Comp Eliminator NHRA Southern Nationals. Don Smith—NHRA Pro Stock Truck NHRA Advance Auto Parts Nationals. Scott Perin—Pro Stock Truck NHRA Lucas Nationals.
2004: Dave Connolly—Pro Stock NHRA Car Quest Auto Parts Nationals, Lucas Nationals, Fall Nationals.
2005: Dave Connolly—Pro Stock NHRA Winternationals, Las Vegas Nationals.
2006: Jim Yates Pro Stock NHRA Pontiac Performance Nationals. Dave Connolly—Pro Stock NHRA Southern Nationals.
2010: Charlie Greco—Comp Eliminator NHRA SPORTSnationals.
Bill had ties to 8 NHRA Championships and 67 NHRA National event wins (excluding 3 Winston Invitational Wins).

Bill Jenkins Awards and Honors

1972: AARWBA Hall of Fame.
1984: Chevrolets Legend of Performance.
1993: Don Garlits Drag Racing Hall of Fame.
1994: EMPA Hall of Fame.
1995: *Super Stock & Drag Illustrated* Hall of Fame.
1996: Motorsports Hall of Fame of America.
2001: Number-8 on NHRA's list of 50 Greatest Drivers.
2008: International Motorsports Hall of Fame.

***Car Craft* Magazine All Star Drag Team Awards**

Bill Jenkins' 20 career All Star Awards is second only

*Ken Dondero got the jump on John Hagen during a AHRA Grand American race at Minnesota Dragway. Ken captured the AHRA Pro Stock Championship with the Monza after starting the year off in **Grumpy's Toy X**.* (Photo Courtesy John Eichinger)

to Don Garlits' 21. The 10 different categories in which Bill won the awards is also a record number.

1967: Super Stock driver, Stock engine builder.
1968: Super Stock driver, Stock engine builder.
1969: Super Stock driver, Super Stock engine builder, Stock engine builder.
1970: Pro Stock driver, Pro Stock engine builder, Super Stock engine builder, Man of the Year.
1972: Pro Stock driver, Pro Stock engine builder.
1973: Pro Stock Driver.
1974: Pro Stock driver.
1975: Pro Stock crew chief.
1976: Pro Stock driver
1977: Pro Stock crew chief.
1978: Pro Stock crew chief, Pro Stock engine builder.

Jenkins Competition Banners

Through 1963: Cars were labeled "Tuned by Bill Jenkins."
Late 1963, 1964, and into 1965: Square logo, black backing with yellow lettering.
Late 1965 to 1966: "Jenkins Competition" in a Chevrolet-blue Bowtie.
1966 to 1968: "Jenkins Competition" in a Chevrolet Bowtie (multiple colors).
1969-up: Chevrolet Bowtie replaced with "Jenkins Competition" inside an arrow.

*The Jenkins Competition logo was a spinoff of the 1965 **Black Arrow** design and is still used.* (Author Collection)

Index

A

AHRA winter meet, 39–42, 52, 65, 70, 74, 75, 115, 118, 121, 124, 126, 127, 138, 140, 141, 145, 147
Allen, Ray, 154, 156–159
Allen, Charlie, 54
Allison, Donnie, 127
Aquasco Raceway, 32, 64, 69, 74
Archbault, John, 96
ATCO Raceway, 101, 123, 133
Auxier, Jr., Sam, 78, 81, 90
Azevedo, Lorry, 120

B

Bakersfield, 70
Beaver Springs dragstrip, 29
Beeline Dragway, Arizona, 41, 52, 118
Beswick, Arnie "The Farmer," 148
Beyer, Ed, 71
Booth, Wally, 68, 139
Bown, Chuck, 163
Brannan, Dick, 22, 42
Brinkley, Larry, 29
Bristol, Tennessee, 67
Brooklyn Heavy, 135
Brookshire, Harold, 112
Brown, Bob, 13, 14, 68
Burgess, Robert "Doc," 49–54
Busch Grand National Goodys 300, 163

C

Cagnazzi, Victor, 167, 168
Cahill, Bob, 39, 52
Campbell, Bill, 24
Carlton, Don, 81, 113, 134, 135
Carpenter, Al, 125
Cayuga Raceway, 146, 149, 153
Cecil County, 29, 38, 42, 43, 47, 48, 51, 54, 56, 61, 64, 66, 74, 76
Chapel, John, 29
Christie, Dave, 126, 139, 145
Cones, Carroll, 22
Connelly, Dave, 168, 169
Cox, Carol, 24
Cox, Joe, 57, 59
Cureton, George, 71, 72, 76
Czerw, Leon, 35

D

Dallas International Motor Speedway, 90, 92, 167
Daytona, 55, 127, 163
Dazzo, Paul, 142
Delorenzo, Joe, 55
Detroit Dragway, 77
Detroit Raceway, 81
Dismuke, Bill "Farmer," 12
Doll, Darwin, 12, 29, 85
Dondero, Ken, 116, 124–127, 139–141, 145, 161, 162, 173
Dragway 42, 123

E

Easy Street Dragstrip, 18
Evans, Clarence, 12, 68, 69

F

Faubel, Bud, 14, 28, 38, 39, 41, 43, 45, 46, 48–50
Ferrara, Dennis, 106, 108
Fezell, Don and Mary Ann, 35
Fields, Truman, 120
Fissel, Don, 67
Fons, Mike, 78, 134
Fontana Raceway, 24
Foss, Mary Ann, 68

G

Gapp & Roush, 121, 123, 124, 133, 134, 136
Gapp, Wayne, 133, 134
Gardner, Joe "Tex," 35, 37, 45, 46
Garlits, Don, 46, 115, 134, 141
Gay, Don, 36
Glidden, Bob, 116, 123, 134, 144–146, 151, 152, 156
Good, John, 12–14
Grotheer, Don, 68, 113, 116
Grove, Tom, 45, 78, 81, 91, 93, 96, 97, 102, 142–145
Guffey, Mike, 48

H

Hall, Jim, 76
Harropp, Bob, 46
Harvey, Paul, 68
Harvey, Jerry, 80
Hedrick, Ed, 70, 72, 74–76, 78, 86–88, 91, 94, 95
Hielscher, "Mr. Bardahl" Bill, 78
Hill, Roy, 132, 135
Holtz, Bill, 14
Hopkinson, Jim, 78
Housey, Dick, 49, 51, 52, 54
Hurley, Frank, 21, 50
Hutchinson, Pete, 113, 130, 131

I

Iaconio, Frank, 144, 157
IHRA, 141, 147, 151, 155, 157, 161
Indianapolis Raceway Park, 24, 25, 36, 54, 107, 115
Irwindale, 112
Island Dragway, 88, 161
Ivo, Tommy, 46
Izykowski, Bill, 85

J

Jarrell, Alex, 57, 71, 79
Johns, Steve, 155–157, 161, 163–168
Johnson, Warren "The Professor," 102, 108, 122, 124, 139, 140
Joneic, Al, 73

K

Kaiser, Bob, 164
Kanners, Dave, 122, 123, 134, 135
Kanuika, Steve, 82
Karamesines, Chris "The Greek," 24
Kerr, Tom, 63, 78
Keystone, 122
Kimball, Gary, 70, 71
Kopp, Larry, 167

L

Lamb, Roger, 129, 130, 138
Landy, Dandy Dick, 78, 81, 84, 115, 116, 127
Lawrence, Dink, 58, 59
Lawton, Bill, 48
Leal, Butch, 116, 121, 123
Lepone, Jr., Joe, 154–162, 165, 166
Lindamood, Roger, 52
Loehr, Dick, 81
Lombardo, Larry, 91, 113, 114, 117, 123, 125, 134, 138–146, 148, 149, 151, 155, 156
Lupo, Frank, 48

M

Mancini, Ron, 68
Maple Grove, 78, 81, 91, 93, 96, 97, 102, 142–145
Martin, Buddy, 46, 47, 68, 75–78, 81, 84, 93, 101, 108, 118, 124
Martini, John, 56
Maskin & Kanners, 122, 135
Maskin, Richard, 145
Mason Dixon Dragoway, 40
McCandless, Herb, 81, 115, 116, 121
McCready, Harold, 135, 136
McDade, Stu, 112
McFarland, Jim, 69
McLaughlin, Dick, 13, 14
Mentzer, Doug, 59
Minnesota Dragway, 173
Montgomery, George, 46

N

Nancy, Tony, 46
Nelson, Larry, 120
Ness, Don, 156
New England Dragway, 109
New York International Raceway, 63
New York Dover Dragstrip, 49, 52, 53
NHRA Gatornationals, 81, 95, 116, 119, 120, 139, 140, 149
NHRA O'Reilly Fallnationals, 167
NHRA Springnationals, 58, 67, 87, 90–92, 95, 132, 135, 144, 146, 155, 167
NHRA Summernationals, 24, 109, 111, 114, 115, 120, 121, 134, 135, 139, 144, 147, 151, 152, 161
NHRA TOYO Nationals, 168
NHRA U.S Nationals, 91, 93, 115, 118,

Index

139, 143, 146, 151, 155, 157
NHRA Winternationals, 21–24, 41, 42, 49–53, 68, 73, 78, 80, 81, 85, 86, 99, 101, 103, 104, 110–113, 117, 118, 120, 121, 124, 138, 141, 145, 150, 152, 155, 160, 162
NHRA World Finals, 65, 70, 72, 74, 75, 80, 87, 88, 116, 126, 139, 158, 161, 162, 166
Nicholson, Don, 18, 22, 24, 26, 27, 43, 68, 76, 78, 82, 105, 109, 116, 123, 125, 136, 143, 144, 151
Northrop, Dave, 168
Numidia Dragway, 89, 129

O

Olster, Al, 67, 97
Orange County International Raceway (OCIR), 78, 81, 85, 101, 126
Oswega, 142, 143

P

Panella, Bob, 160–162
Paunch, Marvin, 48
Piggins, Vince, 18, 63, 66, 90, 127
Pitman, K. S., 46
Pittsburgh International Dragway, 28, 48, 108, 124, 127, 135
Pizzi, Tony, 43, 55, 57, 61
Platt, Hubert, 68, 81
Preston, Pete, 58, 59, 70
Prior, Paul, 63, 66, 99
Proffitt, Hayden, 19, 22, 24, 41

Q

Quay, Ed, 120, 122, 129

R

Raceway Park, 25, 152
Riffle, Bob, 120

S

Schartman, Fast Eddie, 135
Schrader, Ken, 163
Seisler, Paul, 87
Shafiroff, Scott, 134, 136
Sharp, Glen, 37, 136
Signorelli, Joe and Marty, 161
Sinistri, Roger, 91
Smith, Ammon R., 15–18, 21, 22, 25, 28, 29, 35, 47, 60, 62, 65, 66, 74, 78, 85, 86, 88, 99, 101, 105, 126
Smith, Lee, 95
Snedon, Tom, 52
Sox & Martin, 46, 47, 68, 75–78, 81, 84, 93, 101, 118, 124
Sox, Ronnie, 32, 43, 46, 47, 67, 69, 75, 78, 82, 108, 117, 124, 134, 136, 160
Spanako, Andy, 55
Spanakos, Bill (Spider), 55, 56, 58, 72
Sperry, Ron, 111, 112
Spidel, Bill, 54
Spiedel, Carl, 51
Stahl, Jere, 33, 39, 43, 57, 60–64, 68, 69, 74, 78, 86
Stepp, Bill, 81, 112, 127, 145
Stiles, Bill, 90, 105
Strickler, Dave, 14–48, 51, 62, 65, 68, 75, 76, 78, 85, 87–89, 94, 96, 99, 102–104
Super Stock Nationals, 54, 63, 70, 77, 78, 91, 94, 97, 98
Swaim, Mike, 163

T

Terry, Ed, 68, 119, 120
The Dodge Boys, 38–48, 51
Thompson, Joe Ralph, 92
Thompson, Mickey, 19
Thorley, Doug, 62
Thornton, Jim, 143
Thurlby, Bub, 143
Toronto Motorsport Park, 153
Trost, Jack, 127, 132, 140
Tryson, Joe, 36, 43, 45, 61, 63, 66, 74, 80, 139, 140, 143, 145, 159, 165
Tucker, Bruce, 63, 64, 67, 69, 70, 72, 73, 77, 88
Tulsa World Finals, 65, 75, 80, 87, 88, 115, 116

V

Van Valkenburgh, Paul, 77
Vanke, Arlen, 19, 29, 68, 70, 75, 93, 97
Vargo Dragway, 65
Vineland Raceway, 30, 32, 35
Volpe, Carlo "Ollie," 55, 60
Von Bargen, Derrick, 110, 113

W

Waldman, Arnie, 36
Wallace & Silman, 118
Warren, Bobby, 65, 72, 87, 139, 140
Watkins, Brad, 79
Weiler, George, 49
Werst, Jack, 55
Whalen, George, 48
Wheatley, Jay and Buck, 79, 81
Whitman, Dick, 100, 110, 113, 130
Wyble, Harry, 88

Y

Yates, Jim, 168
Yenko, 59, 94, 95, 97
York US-30 Dragway, 11, 12, 14, 16–20, 22, 24, 27–29, 31–33, 43, 49, 52, 53, 56, 58, 62, 63, 67, 75, 77, 78, 82, 91, 93, 97–99, 133, 134, 136, 148, 161
Yowell, Bobby, 145

Z

Zul, Richie, 106, 108, 121

Additional books that may interest you...

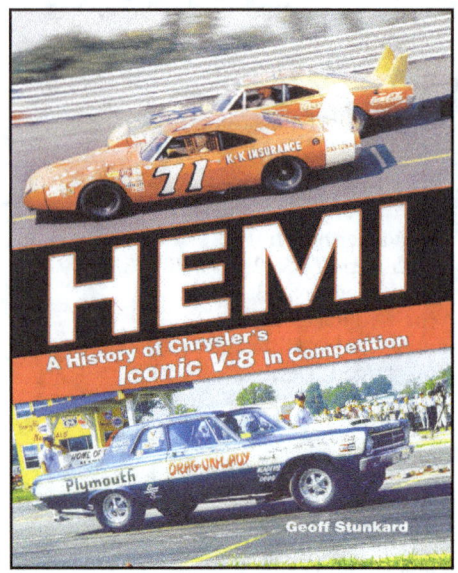

HEMI: A History of Chrysler's Iconic V-8 In Competition by Geoff Stunkard In the pages of this comprehensive Hemi history, the author goes behind the scenes and reveals how the engine was designed, built, tested, and eventually raced. He follows the engine as it rewrote racing history, became a highly sought-after engine in street cars, and redefined V-8 performance. Whether the Hemi was installed in a Charger, Super Bee, Baracuda, Superbird, or other car, it dominated in NHRA, NASCAR, and other forms of competition. The racing triumphs of Richard Petty, David Pearson, Dick Landy, Don Garlits, and countless others are brought back to life. Hardbound, 8.5 x 11 inches, 192 pages, 400 color photos. *Item # CT537*

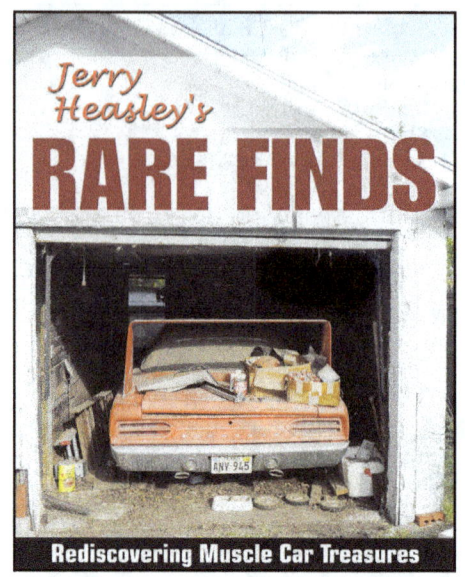

JERRY HEASLEY'S RARE FINDS by Jerry Heasley Jerry Heasley's Rare Finds column has been revealing the fascinating exploits of collectors unearthing exotic muscle cars for years. In these fantastic tales, years of detective work, research, and countless phone calls culminate in rediscovery and reclaiming of rare classic muscle cars. Heasley's evocative prose and on-the-scene photographs bring these unique, challenging, and fascinating automotive adventures to life. Forgotten, unrecognized, and underappreciated cars have been found in barns, fields, and packed away in garages for years waiting for an enthusiast to return them to their former glory. Some tales are so extraordinary they defy belief. Softbound, 8.5 x 11 inches, 144 pages, 235 color photos. *Item # CT497*

STREET SLEEPERS: The Art of the Deceptively Fast Car by Tommy Lee Byrd The art of building a successful sleeper has varied over the decades as styles and times have changed. One fact that remains constant is that the car's appearance belies its performance potential. This book exposes those secrets, and the owners and builders of some of America's quickest street machines share their deceptive art. Outstanding photography and in-depth owner interviews tell the tale, and even engine specifications and quarter-mile track times are shared. There was a time when such things were well-guarded secrets, but this book truly exposes all the tricks! The photos in this edition are black & white. Softbound, 8.5 x 11 inches, 144 pages, 321 b/w photos. *Item # CT498P*

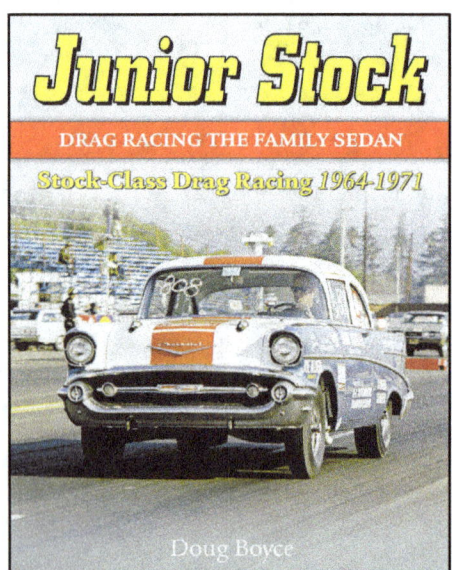

JUNIOR STOCK: Drag Racing the Family Sedan by Doug Boyce In the 1950s and 1960s, drag racing was an exciting new sport that anyone with a car could participate in. Based on their equipment, the participants' cars were assigned to specific classes. This class format encouraged amateur participation on a level never before seen. Stock-class drag racing is celebrated in this book, with hundreds of vintage color photographs showing the way it used to be. If you were a fan or participant back in the day, or are a lover of vintage drag cars, *Junior Stock: Drag Racing the Family Sedan* is a book you are sure to thoroughly enjoy. Softbound, 8.5 x 11 inches, 176 pages, 458 color photos. *Item # CT505*

TOP FUEL DRAGSTERS by Steve Reyes Over the course of the evolution of technological developments in the late 1960s and early 1970s, Top Fuelers were making enough horsepower so that sitting directly behind the engine, as the "diggers" did in the 1950s through the 1960s, was recognized as a fairly dangerous proposition. Any blower explosion or clutch and bellhousing failure occurred directly in the face of the pilot. Teams and engineers developed the rear-engine layout that is still in use today, where the engine sits behind the driver but in front of the rear wheels. Industry legend journalist Steve Reyes was there through all the technological changes; he has the photos, anecdotes, quotes, and tales of the era. Join him in the pages of this book where he shares all the stories of this incredible racing era. Softbound, 8.5 x 11 inches, 176 pages, 300 images. *Item # CT547*

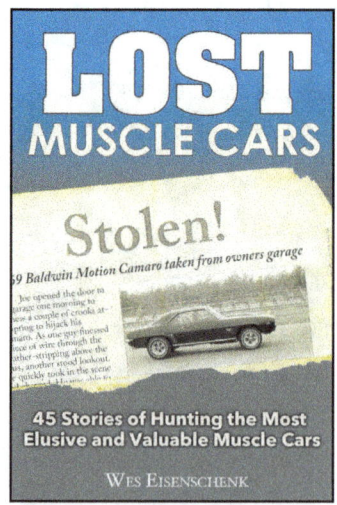

LOST MUSCLE CARS by Wes Eisenschenk This book is a collection of stories written by enthusiasts about their quest to find these extremely rare and valuable muscle cars. The four categories (Celebrity, Rare, Race Cars, and Concept/Prototype/Show Cars) within three genres (Missing, Lost History, Recently Discovered) take you through the search for some of the most sought after muscle cars with names including Shelby, Yenko, Hurst, and Hemi. Hardbound 6 x 9 inches, 256 pages, 100 photos. *Item # CT551*

www.cartechbooks.com or 1-800-551-4754

www.ingramcontent.com/pod-product-compliance
Lightning Source LLC
Chambersburg PA
CBHW051407070526
44584CB00023B/3328